The United Nations
A Beginner's Guide

ONEWORLD BEGINNER'S GUIDES combine an original, inventive, and engaging approach with expert analysis on subjects ranging from art and history to religion and politics, and everything in between. Innovative and affordable, books in the series are perfect for anyone curious about the way the world works and the big ideas of our time.

Beginners
GUIDES

The United Nations
A Beginner's Guide

Norrie MacQueen

ONEWORLD
OXFORD

A Oneworld Paperback Original

Published by Oneworld Publications 2010

Copyright © Norrie MacQueen 2010

The right of Norrie MacQueen to be identified as the Author
of this work has been asserted by him in accordance with
the Copyright, Designs and Patents Act 1988

ISBN 978–1–85168–752–7

Typeset by Jayvee, Trivandrum, India
Cover design by Simon McFadden
Printed and bound by CPI Cox & Wyman, Reading, RG1 8EX

Oneworld Publications
UK: 185 Banbury Road, Oxford, OX2 7AR, England
USA: 38 Greene Street, 4th Floor, New York, NY 10013, USA
www.oneworld-publications.com

Contents

List of illustrations

Abbreviations and acronyms

CBD	Convention on Biological Diversity
CDM	Clean Development Mechanism
ECOSOC	Economic and Social Council
EEZ	Exclusive Economic Zone (Convention of the Law of the Sea)
FAO	Food and Agriculture Organization
HDI	Human Development Index (UNDP)
IAEC	International Atomic Energy Commission
IBRD	International Bank for Reconstruction and Development (the World Bank)
ICC	International Criminal Court
ICJ	International Court of Justice
IDP	Internally displaced person
IFAD	International Fund for Agricultural Development
IGO	Inter-governmental organization
ILC	International Law Commission
ILO	International Labour Office (later, Organization)
IMF	International Monetary Fund
INCB	International Narcotics Control Board
IPCC	Intergovernmental Panel on Climate Change
M+5	2005 World Summit (Millennium plus five years)
MDGs	Millennium Development Goals
MSC	Military Staff Committee (of the Security Council)
NATO	North Atlantic Treaty Organization
NGO	Non-Governmental Organization

NIEO	New International Economic Order
NPT	Nuclear Non-Proliferation Treaty (1968)
OCHA	United Nations Office for the Coordination of Humanitarian Affairs
P5	The five permanent members of the Security Council (Britain, France, Russia, China and the United States)
R2P	The Responsibility to Protect (intervention doctrine placing responsibility on UN forces for the protection of civilians, using force if necessary)
SALT	Strategic Arms Limitation Talks
SAP	Structural Adjustment Programme (schemes of financial and economic reform imposed on countries by the Bretton Woods institutions)
UDHR	Universal Declaration of Human Rights
UNCTAD	United Nations Conference on Trade and Development
UNDP	United Nations Development Programme
UNEF	United Nations Emergency Force (deployed after the Suez crisis of 1956)
UNEP	United Nations Environment Programme
UNESCO	United Nations Educational, Scientific and Cultural Organization
UNFCCC	United Nations Framework Convention on Climate Control
UNHCR	United Nations High Commission for Refugees
UNICEF	United Nations Children's (Emergency) Fund
UNIFIL	United Nations Interim Force in Lebanon
UNMD	United Nations Millennium Declaration
WMO	World Meteorological Organization

Members of the United Nations

1945

Argentina
Australia
Belarus
Belgium
Bolivia
Brazil
Canada
Chile
China
Colombia
Costa Rica
Cuba
Czechoslovakia
Denmark
Dominican
  Republic
Ecuador
Egypt
El Salvador
Ethiopia
France
Greece
Guatemala
Haiti
Honduras
India
Iran
Iraq
Lebanon
Liberia
Luxembourg
Mexico
Netherlands
New Zealand
Nicaragua
Norway
Panama
Paraguay
Peru
Philippines
Poland
Saudi Arabia
South Africa
Syria
Turkey
Ukraine
United Kingdom
United States
Uruguay
USSR
Venezuela
Yugoslavia

1946

Afghanistan
Iceland
Sweden
Thailand

1947

Pakistan
Yemen

1948

Burma

1949

Israel

1950

Indonesia

1955

Albania

Austria
Bulgaria
Cambodia
Finland
Hungary
Ireland
Italy
Jordan
Laos
Libya
Nepal
Portugal
Romania
Spain
Sri Lanka

1956

Ghana
Japan
Morocco
Sudan
Tunisia

1957

Malaysia

1958

Guinea

1960

Benin
Burkina Faso

Cameroon
Central African
    Republic
Chad
Congo Brazzaville
Côte d'Ivoire
Cyprus
DR Congo
Gabon
Madagascar
Mali
Niger
Nigeria
Senegal
Somalia
Togo

1961

Mauritania
Mongolia
Sierra Leone
Tanzania

1962

Algeria
Burundi
Jamaica
Rwanda
Trinidad and Tobago
Uganda

1963

Kenya

Kuwait
Zanzibar

1964

Malawi
Malta
Zambia

1965

Gambia
Maldives
Singapore

1966

Barbados
Botswana
Guyana
Lesotho

1967

Democratic
    Yemen

1968

Equatorial Guinea
Mauritius
Swaziland

1970

Fiji

1971

Bahrain
Bhutan
Oman
Qatar
United Arab
  Emirates

1973

Bahamas
Germany (Federal
  Republic)
Germany
  (Democratic
  Republic)

1974

Bangladesh
Grenada
Guinea-Bissau

1975

Cape Verde
Comoros
Mozambique
Papua New
  Guinea
Sao Tome and
  Principe
Suriname

1976

Angola
Samoa
Seychelles

1977

Djibouti
Vietnam

1978

Dominica
Solomon Islands

1979

Saint Lucia

1980

Saint Vincent and
  the Grenadines
Zimbabwe

1981

Antigua and
  Barbuda
Belize
Vanuatu

1983

Saint Kitts and Nevis

1984

Brunei

1990

Liechtenstein
Namibia

1991

Estonia
Latvia
Lithuania
Marshall Islands
Micronesia
North Korea
South Korea

1992

Armenia
Azerbaijan
Bosnia and
  Herzegovina
Croatia
Georgia
Kazakhstan
Kyrgyzstan
Moldova
San Marino
Slovenia
Tajikistan
Turkmenistan

Uzbekistan

1993

Andorra
Czech
  Republic
Eritrea
Macedonia
Monaco
Slovakia

1994

Palau

1999

Kiribati
Nauru
Tonga

2000

Tuvalu

Yugoslavia (revised
  boundarues)

2002

Switzerland
Timor Leste

2006

Montenegro

United Nations peace-keeping operations since 1948

1948–present	Palestine
1949–present	Kashmir
1956–1967	Suez
1958	Lebanon
1960–1964	Congo
1962–1963	West New Guinea
1963–1964	Yemen
1964–present	Cyprus
1965–1966	Dominican Republic
1965–1966	India–Pakistan
1973–1979	Sinai
1974–present	Golan Heights
1978–present	Lebanon
1988–1990	Afghanistan–Pakistan
1988–1991	Iran–Iraq
1988–1999	Angola
1989–1990	Namibia
1989–1992	Central America
1991–1993	Cambodia
1991–1995	El Salvador
1991–2003	Iraq–Kuwait
1991–present	Western Sahara
1992–1994	Mozambique
1992–1995	Somalia
1992–1999	Macedonia

1992–2002	Bosnia
1992–2002	Croatia
1993–1994	Uganda–Rwanda
1993–1996	Rwanda
1993–present	Georgia
1993–present	Haiti
1993–present	Liberia
1994	Chad–Libya
1994–2000	Tajikistan
1997	Guatemala
1998–2000	Central African Republic
1998–2005	Sierra Leone
1999–present	DR Congo
1999–present	East Timor
1999–present	Kosovo
2000–2008	Ethiopia–Eritrea
2004–2006	Burundi
2004–present	Côte d'Ivoire
2005–present	Sudan
2007–present	Central African Republic–Chad
2007–present	Darfur

1

The origins of the UN

When the United Nations was formed in 1945 it did not come out of the blue. It was simply the latest stage in a long process in international politics with beginnings stretching far back in world history. The idea of organized, long term cooperation between political communities was present in the Greek city state system as early as the fifth century BCE. An informal league, formed initially to protect religious sites, gradually took on the character of an international organization with a role in conflict resolution and even collective security among the independent states of the Hellenic peninsula. The United Nations of today then is just the current incarnation of a creature which has existed in some form for millennia.

The more modern pedigree of the UN can be tracked back to Europe in the mid-seventeenth century. In 1648 the dreadful Thirty Years War, which had laid waste to large parts of north-ern continental Europe since its outbreak in 1618, ended with the signing of the Treaty of Westphalia. The aftermath of subse-quent major conflicts – themselves markers of the breakdown of international relations – brought their own designs to make the international system work.

Historical traces: from Westphalia to the Concert of Europe

In its effort to remove the causes of the Thirty Years War, the Treaty of Westphalia set out what would become the basic principles of contemporary international relations. The three key concepts advanced at Westphalia were territoriality, sovereignty and autonomy. Henceforward international politics was to be conducted on the basis of territorially defined states with fixed geographic borders between them. Within these borders government would be sovereign; the state would have unqualified political and legal power in its own space. These nation-states would be autonomous from each and there would be an uncrossable division between domestic and external politics.

It seems odd perhaps that this emphasis on state power and independence could be a key stage in the development of international organization, which implies a breaking down of divisions and restraints on national power and sovereignty. But the establishment of a state based international system composed of autonomous governments was a fundamental prerequisite for the creation of effective inter-governmental organizations (IGOs), of which the United Nations is the most developed model to date. The Westphalian system replaced the remnants of the old idea of Christendom in Europe which had been based on the notion of overarching religious authority transcending that of local politics. By the beginning of the seventeenth century the Protestant Reformation in northern Europe had challenged the idea of universal religious obedience. Simultaneously, far-reaching social and economic changes undermined the old feudal system of political power. Together, these two forces of modernization created such strains on the international relations of the time that their breakdown in general conflict became inevitable. The eventual resolution of this conflict at Westphalia then set the terms for modern world politics. The political arrangement in Europe after 1648 created the conditions for the emergence of a new international society based on cooperation – however limited and self-interested. Paradoxically therefore the essential conditions for international cooperation and organization grew out of a new emphasis on independence and sovereignty.

The Peace of Westphalia proved to be the first turn of a cycle which was maintained over the next three centuries right up to the establishment of the United Nations in 1945. The phases in this cycle went like this:

1. Pressures would build within international politics and eventually bring about breakdown in the form of general war.
2. The end of this war would generate attempts to regulate the new post-war system in ways that would meet the specific problems which had brought about the breakdown.
3. At each turn of the cycle the new regulatory mechanisms would be more elaborate and would require a higher level of cooperation than the previous one.

The end of the Thirty Years War began the process by creating the basic rules of the new system. The next breakdown comparable to the Thirty Years War came with the system-wide wars in the decades after the French Revolution at the end of the eighteenth century. The Congress of Vienna in 1815 and later treaties which set the character of the post-1815 international system performed roughly the same function as Westphalia had in 1648. Now, though, the regulatory mechanism required a higher commitment from the major actors in the system. The victorious powers would now be more proactive in overseeing the workings of the post-war system. It was no longer enough merely to set out ground-rules; they had to be positively imposed. The result was the 'Concert of Europe' composed of the big powers – Britain, Prussia, Austria, Russia – which had defeated revolutionary France. The balance of power would now be actively managed and military intervention used where necessary to maintain it. To this end, regular gatherings of national representatives were held which attempted to negotiate conflicts in the system rather than allow them to spill into violence. And the concert system was, in retrospect, successful in managing relations between states, even if its fundamental conservatism had a deadening effect on progressive politics within them.

Interestingly, Henry Kissinger drew on the model of the Concert system when as US secretary of state in the 1970s he set about constructing the détente between the superpowers which brought, however temporarily, an easing of Cold War tensions. An academic before becoming a practitioner, Kissinger's early research had been into the post-1815 Concert system. As a committed realist, Kissinger thoroughly approved – as indicated in the title of his first book, published in 1957, which explored the Concert system: *A World Restored*. Kissinger's belief was that the major powers in the world at any point – whether in 1815 or in 1970 – were bound together by a mutual self-interest in maintaining stability in the international system. Instability, after all, posed a threat to their dominance. To this extent all big powers were conservative powers whatever the colour of their internal politics. Consequently, on the international plane, the strongest states should actively cooperate to manage global relations regardless of any ideological differences there might be between them. This applied just as much to the United States, the Soviet Union and China in his day as it did to Britain, Austria-Hungary and Prussia in the first half of the nineteenth century.

Clearly this was still a long way from the degree of international cooperation associated with the modern United Nations. It was also based on the active management of a balance of power rather than the replacement of balance of power politics with global collectivism. But the Concert system, with its implicit acknowledgement that peace could only be maintained by active management, was a step towards it.

The Concert system was reasonably successful in maintaining peace in Europe through the stresses and strains of much of the nineteenth century. There was no major conflict between the major powers until the Crimean War in the 1850s, and even this did not prefigure a general breakdown in European relations. Other factors though also accelerated the long march towards the United Nations. The rapid technological advances of the later nineteenth century, particularly in transport and communications, were crucial. International cooperation was enormously aided by the development of the European rail network and the invention of telegraphy. Big set-piece international conferences – such as those in Berlin in the 1870s and 1880s dealing with the Balkans and with the European scramble for Africa – could be quickly and efficiently organized. National leaders could meet face-to-face in a way unthinkable even a few decades before. At the same time, the dark side of technical innovation – the increased mechanization of war fighting – led to unprecedented international attempts to control the spread of new destructive weapons. The Hague Disarmament Conferences of 1899 and 1907 were ultimately unsuccessful. The self-denying ordinances that would be required were simply too much to ask of European states at the height of their imperial pomp. But despite this, the Hague talks did mark yet another step towards modern international organization.

THE HISTORICAL CYCLE OF INTERNATIONAL REGULATION

System breakdown	Settlement	Regulation
Thirty Years War	Westphalia (1648)	State Sovereignty
Napoleonic Wars	Vienna (1815)	Concert of Europe
First World War	Versailles (1919)	League of Nations
Second World War	San Francisco (1945)	United Nations

The League of Nations

The failure of the Hague Conferences – and more broadly of the post-1815 cycle of international regulation – was horrifically confirmed by the outbreak of the First World War in 1914. But its end in 1918 brought the latest turn of the stress–war–regulation cycle. However, emerging from the Treaty of Versailles, there was a quantum leap in the nature of regulation: the new League of Nations. This would be the world's first IGO, properly speaking, in that it had a global membership which was required to sign up to a constitution and meet together regularly at a permanent location in order to pursue the objectives of the institution. The principal architect of this new organization was the American Democratic president Woodrow Wilson.

However radical the ideas behind it, the creation of the League of Nations could not be said to have taken the world wholly by surprise. The expectation that new forms of international management would follow major conflicts was now a familiar one and the First World War had been of such traumatic proportions that a particularly bold approach was inevitable. Even beyond this, though, an intellectual climate had developed on both sides of the Atlantic at the beginning of the twentieth century in which new and unashamedly modernist ideas for global regulation flourished. In part this was a result of the influence of the new social sciences. The idea that scientific solutions to problems need not be restricted to the physical world was gaining currency. Economics had been growing as a discipline since the eighteenth century, of course, but now figures as diverse as Karl Marx and Sigmund Freud were laying claims to an extension of scientific analysis and prescription to a much wider range of social problems. And what social problem could be more demanding of scientific solution than that of international war?

Even before the outbreak of the war the French social theorist Léon Bourgeois had proposed that the radical seventeenth-century idea of the social contract – setting out the relationship of rights and obligations of peoples and their governments – could be extended from the domestic to the international level. Individual countries, Bourgeois argued, could and should contract into a general agreement with the collective of world states, undertaking to accept certain responsibilities in return for the guarantee of rights and protections. The result would be a peaceful and secure global environment. Simultaneously, on the other side of the Atlantic, similar ideas were being advocated, though here they reflected America's constitutional political culture by emphasizing legal structures more than philosophical propositions. The League to Enforce Peace, led by former president William Howard Taft, proposed a permanent 'parliament' of states which would draw its authority from a world court.

Unsurprisingly, it was this American perspective that shaped the thinking of Woodrow Wilson. The son of a Presbyterian minister, Wilson's moral compass had been set early in life. He had first pursued an academic career, rising to become president of Princeton University. From this prominent position he entered politics and was eventually invited to run as Democratic presidential candidate. Following success in the 1912 election he took office in 1913. His sense of moral responsibility led him, against considerable political and public opposition, to bring the United States into the war on the allied side in 1917, 'that the world be made safe for democracy' as he put it in his address seeking the support of the legislature. In January 1918 he delivered his famous Fourteen Points to the US Congress which set out America's war aims. The last of these called for the creation of a 'general association of nations' to be 'formed under specific covenants for the purpose of affording mutual guarantees of political independence and territorial integrity to great and small states alike'.[1] The foundations of the latest cycle of post-conflict regulation – and the template for contemporary global organization – were thus laid. America's dominant position at the Versailles negotiations in 1919 as the least damaged and by far the most powerful of the victorious powers, ensured that the League would come into being, even if the final outcome was not quite as Wilson himself had foreseen.

The new League was a profoundly revolutionary innovation in a number of respects. Its structure and functions set the standard for the range of international organizations which followed across the twentieth century. This was most strikingly so in relation to the United Nations, its direct successor. The ambitions of the League went far beyond those of the old Concert of Europe. The League was the first international organization to be built around a formal statement of principles and objectives. In other words, and reflecting the legalistic instincts of its principal advocate, it had a constitution: the Covenant (a direct echo from Wilson's Fourteenth Point). The League was also the first international organization to have a permanent headquarters, the Palais des Nations in Geneva (today the European headquarters of the United Nations). Another revolutionary innovation was the creation of a permanent, dedicated bureaucracy (or secretariat) overseen by a secretary-general (originally with the title of Chancellor). Uniquely, the international civil servants who made up this secretariat, although drawn from the member states, were to be loyal primarily to the League and not to their home countries. The League was to operate on the basis of a quasi-state structure. The secretariat approximated to a national civil service, of course, but there was also to be a semi-executive Council composed of the major powers, and a semi-parliamentary Assembly which would represent the membership as a whole. And, the structure would embrace a Permanent Court of International Justice which would be located in The Hague.

The deeply radical character of this new organization is perhaps not fully appreciated today. In part this is due simply to the fact

Figure 1 Palais des Nations, Geneva, Seat of the League of Nations and later the European Headquarters of the United Nations (UN Photo)

that the League set the template for a plethora of later organizations whose structures are now routinely familiar to us. But in part it is due to the general perception that the League was a historic failure on the grandest of scales and that little about it is worth commemorating. There was, after all, a Second World War.

The inescapable fact is that the League's central purpose was not realized. The League of Nations existed first and foremost to oversee a global system of collective security. Beyond all the radical innovations in its structure and operations this was to be its unique advance on the regulatory attempts which had followed the conflicts before the First World War. With the advent of the League states were no longer supposed to be wholly responsible for their own security in relation to other states in the international system. Security was to be collectivized by the system as a whole, with the League of Nations presiding over this new multilateral framework. At the outset the Covenant required League members to accept 'obligations not to resort to war'. It then insisted 'that the maintenance of peace requires the reduction of national armaments to the lowest point consistent with national safety and the enforcement by common action of international obligations'. National weapon stocks were thus to be maintained only at a level which would allow the state to preserve order and, crucially, to contribute to the imposition of collective security beyond its frontiers. League members were 'to respect and preserve as against external aggression the territorial integrity and existing political independence' of all other members, and the Council, as its executive organ, would 'advise upon the means by which this obligation will be fulfilled'. Any 'war or threat of war whether immediately affecting any of the Members of the League or not [was] a matter of concern to the whole League' which would 'take any action that may be deemed wise and effectual to safeguard the peace of nations'.[2]

ORIGINAL MEMBERS OF THE LEAGUE OF NATIONS IN 1920

Albania Argentina Australia Austria Belgium Bolivia Brazil British Empire Bulgaria Canada Chile China Colombia Costa Rica Cuba Czechoslovakia Denmark Finland France Greece Guatemala Haiti Honduras Iran Italy Japan Liberia Luxembourg Netherlands New Zealand Nicaragua Norway Panama Paraguay Peru Poland Portugal Romania El Salvador South Africa Spain Sweden Switzerland Thailand Uruguay Venezuela Yugoslavia

(Germany was admitted in 1926 and left in 1933.
The USSR was admitted in 1934)

The gap between rhetoric and reality, however, was immense. The huge ambitions of the League Covenant, particularly in the critical area of international security, would not be realized. Different explanations have been suggested for this. For one thing, the United States, from where the principal moral vision and the main ideas about the structure for organization had come, did not itself join the League. Wilson, though able to cajole reluctant European allies into accepting his vision at Versailles, proved unable to convince Congress to ratify US membership. A post-war tendency among American politicians towards isolationism (at least from 'old' Europe) proved stronger than the President's missionary fervour for engagement. It has been argued that without the United States to drive it in the proper direction, the League fell under the backsliding leadership of European powers such as Britain and France who had never truly bought into Wilsonian idealism. The European instinct was to manage the League as an extension of the nineteenth century Concert system rather than as a fundamental departure from it. The League, in this view, should be a loose alliance of like-minded states who would quietly manage the balance of power. Crucially in this regard, the League was never a truly universalist organization. Its membership, particularly at the beginning, was restricted. Defeated Germany was excluded from the club. So was the new Soviet Union which lay beyond the pale of 'civilized' countries. With the United States, the League's architect removed from its development and its leadership passed to the less than wholeheartedly committed Europeans, the basic structure, the argument runs, would inevitably collapse sooner or later.

But the flaws in the League's ideas were probably more fundamental. American withdrawal, rather than proving fatal in itself, perhaps just underlined a more fundamental obstacle. The world of 1919 – like the world of 1945 and the world of today – was still organized in a system based on the sovereign state.

Those states would always insist on making their own sovereign decisions and maintaining their own sovereign independence of action, particularly in such a core area as the security of the nation. Wilson's League of Nations, in short, was an idea whose time had still not come. Collective security was seen as incompatible with national security and, quite simply, no independent state would sacrifice the second in pursuit of the first. This was not perhaps immediately evident during the first years of the League's existence. The 1920s was a decade of relative calm in world politics. Perhaps, many felt, international relations could be regulated and perhaps the League, however imperfect, could provide the structure for this. But by the early 1930s the picture was changing. The stability of the 1920s began to appear merely as a temporary, post-traumatic response to the horrors of the First World War rather than the dawn of a new age in world politics.

The new decade brought a sequence of challenges to the League's capacity to deliver collective security – and it appeared to fail each one. In 1931 blatant Japanese aggression towards China in Manchuria went unpunished as the League's European leaders persisted with their traditional, narrowly focused vision of national interest. A similar response met Italy's invasion of the independent African state of Abyssinia (Ethiopia) in 1935. Any measures taken were wholly inadequate and were designed to give the impression of serious intent without running the political risks of real action. The later years of the 1930s were, of course, dominated by acts of aggression by Nazi Germany. By this time, though, there was virtually no international confidence in the League and it rapidly fell into irrelevance.

Yet the failure of collective security in the 1930s has, quite unfairly, overshadowed more general assessments of the League project. The unfairness is twofold. First, any failure lay with the League's leading members – sovereign states – rather than the institution itself. This is more than a semantic quibble.

Throughout the story of the United Nations, as we will see, the organization has persistently been criticized for sins both of commission and omission when critical decisions to act or not to act have been taken, on the basis of self-interest, by its individual member states. In this way the League and later the UN might be criticized at times for unrealistic ambition, but the failure to realize this ambition is ultimately national not institutional. The failures in Somalia and Rwanda in the 1990s are essentially the same as those in China and Abyssinia in the 1930s: the inevitable result of decision-making by states preoccupied with their own perceptions of their own national interests.

The second unfairness common in assessments of the League is the neglect of areas in which it was actually very successful. In the fifteen years or so after the end of the First World War the League was closely and successfully involved in easing into existence the new arrangement of states in Europe which followed the break-up of the German, Austrian and Turkish empires. League officials oversaw popular votes (plebiscites) in disputed border areas and worked to reduce tensions in the transition. Specifically, the League provided a temporary administration for the Free City of Danzig (modern day Gdansk) which had been transferred from Germany to provide Poland with an outlet to the Baltic Sea at the end of the newly created Polish Corridor. More substantially the League administered the disputed Saar territory between Germany and France from 1920 to 1935 when a League international force supervised a League-organized plebiscite (which returned the Saar to German sovereignty). Timely intervention by the League in the early 1930s also forestalled what might have been a disastrous war between Peru and Colombia over a border dispute of the Amazon.

Beyond these, admittedly limited, security related successes, the League of Nations could boast other real achievements by the time of its demise. The mandate system introduced for the overseas colonies of the defeated powers after the war marked a huge step forward in thinking about imperialism. The essence of the new approach was that the imperial possessions removed from the defeated should not simply become, as always in the past, spoils of war for the victors. Instead, the administration of colonies was to be the responsibility of suitable powers until such time as they were ready for independent statehood. A mandate was designed to be an intermediate stage on the way to independence and the mandatory (the state now responsible for the territory) had a duty to prepare its population for this. Here too, Wilsonian morality and American suspicion of old-fashioned European imperialism were evident. The mandate approach was one of the most successful innovations associated with the League of Nations – and one of the many taken over virtually unchanged by the United Nations Trusteeship system (see Chapter 6). In its last years the League began widening its activities into a range of global social and economic concerns which would later be taken over by the UN Economic and Social Council (ECOSOC). It had already provided an umbrella for numerous specialized (or functional) agencies dealing with such issues from the International Labour Office (ILO) to the Universal Postal Union, another responsibility inherited by the UN.

In 1939, however, as the world slid into general war once again, there were few governments or even individuals ready to celebrate these achievements.

Wartime preparations for the United Nations

Despite the collapse of the League's credibility, so embedded had the idea of post-conflict projects for the better regulation of international relations become that there was never any doubt that a new organization would emerge with the peace. This latest revolution of the cycle would maintain the tendency to ever deeper cooperation. This time the vehicle for this would be the United Nations, and plans for its creation were already underway shortly after the outbreak of the Second World War.

In August 1941, two years into the war against Nazi Germany and four months before the Japanese attack on Pearl Harbor was to bring the entry of the United States into the conflict, the American president, Franklin Delano Roosevelt, met the British prime minister, Winston Churchill, on board a warship off the Canadian coast. The outcome of this meeting was the Atlantic Charter. This statement of joint aspirations set the goal of collective security for the post-war world. All 'nations of the world, for realistic as well as spiritual reasons', the Charter stated, 'must come to the abandonment of the use of force'. To this end there should be 'the establishment of a ... permanent system of general security'.[3] The aspiration had been set, though the specifics would be worked out over the follow-ing years of war. Soon after America's entry to the war, however, the term 'United Nations' came into common use. At this point it did not yet refer to an international organization. It was the description that the allied states gave themselves; the war became one between the Axis powers and the United Nations.

As the war slowly turned in the allies' favour, concrete planning for the new organization gained pace. As with the League, the main impetus came from the United States. President Roosevelt's worldview and its moral underpinnings were in many ways similar to those of Woodrow Wilson. But Roosevelt's outlook was in some critical respects more practical. His ethical vision was tempered by a clearer awareness of the realties of world politics than that of his predecessor. And, of course, the League had now come and gone, leaving lessons for the learning. Roosevelt also had the fate of Wilson's grand scheme at the hands of the US Congress to contemplate and was determined to avoid a repeat of the isolationist backlash which had kept America out of the League.

His initial plan was for a system of multilateral security, but one based on the central role of the post-war big powers. These, in addition to the United States itself, would undoubtedly be the Soviet Union and Britain. An Asian dimension might possibly be provided by China, though at this time a brutal Japanese occupation and a continuing civil war between Nationalists and Communists put this in some doubt. The capacity of these powers to act as world policemen, as Roosevelt put it, would be enhanced by a programme of phased disarmament among the other states in the organization (an approach prefigured in the League Covenant).

At the Tehran conference attended by the allies in 1943, Roosevelt's secretary of state Cordell Hull secured a commitment from the Soviet foreign minister Vyacheslav Molotov and British foreign secretary Anthony Eden to the creation of a general international organization based on the principles of sovereign equality. Though resounding, this declaration was somewhat vague if not vacuous. This was probably designed to disguise some serious differences that were beginning to emerge among the allies as the reality – and imminence – of the new organization came home to them. In an echo of the discussions around the League of Nations at Versailles, the Americans pushed for a much further-reaching institution; one which would equip the new United Nations with far greater authority than the League. They urged a positive transfer of power in the organization into the hands of the 'policemen' who would be able to act decisively without being too much troubled by the democratic processes of sovereign independence in the body as a whole. The League's requirement of unanimous votes before action could be taken was seen in Washington as one of the main factors in the failure of inter-war collective security.

If Roosevelt's vision of a powerful centralized United Nations mirrored the position of Wilson in the construction of the League, Churchill's position similarly echoed the script Britain had followed at Versailles. He had a less radical image for the new organization, one which still carried a whiff of nostalgia for the nineteenth century Concert system. Perhaps predictably in view of their contrasting political cultures, Britain and America drew different lessons from the fate of the League. While the American approach looked to more demanding and more tightly defined legal obligations as the way forward, the British were more pragmatic. The League, in their view, had asked not too little but too much of its members. In a system of sovereign states, governments would always conduct foreign policy in what they saw as their own national interests. This could not be changed by a legal formula, as Roosevelt seemed to suggest. Even putting aside the disastrous experience of collective security – or the lack of it – under the League, the smaller states would continue to rely ultimately on their own resources in defence of their own security. They would not surrender this capacity to a cohort of big powers, however well intentioned and however sunny the prospect of peace and security they held out. And, viewed realistically, what about those big powers and their promises? How reliable was their commitment to act in defence of others where no immediate self-interest was involved? The record from Manchuria to Abyssinia offered no reassurance.

From this more cautious starting point the British favoured a less centralized, more regionally based structure for the new organization. Its global dimension should be a loose general structure; it should not be the location of all key decision-making. Importantly, a regional focus would tie national interests to local collective security. The big powers would still have a special role, but only within their own backyards. Britain would have a leadership role in the security of Western Europe and the USSR in Eastern Europe while the United States would be concerned primarily with the western hemisphere. China, assuming it qualified as a big power, would obviously oversee collective security in Asia (at least in those parts that were not components of European empires).

Characteristically, the Soviet position, set by Joseph Stalin, was somewhat opaque and difficult to read. The British model would have consolidated and legitimized Moscow's sphere of interest in Eastern Europe. It would also have helped exclude American interference elsewhere in the world. But, ever sensitive to the dynamics of power, Stalin was aware that it was the American position that was likely to prevail. After the disastrous experience of the infant Soviet Union's isolation following the First World War, he was determined that it should now be at the heart of the new organization, whatever its structure. Consequently, it was the American model with which he finally identified. And, with some elaboration and adjustment, it was the American model which formed the template for the new organization's structures and purposes.

In August 1944, a year after the Tehran meeting and at a point when the allied victory appeared to be more or less inevitable, at least in Europe, a series of meetings began at Dumbarton Oaks near Washington DC. At these talks the Soviet and British ambassadors to the United States (with a Nationalist Chinese delegation present in a lesser capacity) met with US State Department officials to begin putting flesh on the skeleton of the United Nations. The basic architecture of the new organization was easily enough agreed. The model of the League of Nations was simply retained. The League Council of big powers was transmuted into a Security Council. This would have eleven members at the outset, most of them sitting for fixed terms but with an inner core of permanent members who would constitute Roosevelt's big power policemen. These permanent members would have special powers, including that of an individual veto over decisions. The League's quasi-parliamentary organ, the Assembly, evolved into the General Assembly of the UN on which all members were represented on the basis of sovereign equality. The functions and powers of the Secretariat would, in essence, remain unchanged and it would continue to be headed by a secretary-general appointed by the organization's membership.

Though the Dumbarton Oaks meetings were successful in agreeing the basic organization of the new UN, they failed to resolve a number of tricky and politically charged issues around processes. Arguments over the use of the veto in the Security Council and the range of membership of the General Assembly cast a harsh and ominous light over the relationship between what would soon become the two Cold War superpowers. The Soviet Union, intensely aware of its vulnerability in the democratic arithmetic of any new world organization, wanted no conditions on the power of veto in the Security Council. Such highly political disagreements were left to be resolved between the national leaders themselves when Roosevelt, Stalin and Churchill met at Yalta on the Black Sea in February 1945, where, with some difficulty, compromises were agreed (see Chapter 2).

The last stage in the creation of the United Nations took the form of an extended period of meetings between April and June 1945. These were held in San Francisco where representatives from forty-six states met to put the finishing touches to the organization's fundamental constitution, the Charter. This United Nations Conference on International Organization marked the shift in the use of the term from a description of a war-time alliance to the title of the new global institution. The gathering began before the allied victory in Europe and ended while fighting continued in Asia. Poignantly, it took place in the absence of the principal architect of the project. President Roosevelt had died just days before the San Francisco meetings began. The new president, Harry H. Truman, became the guardian of his predecessor's flame, maintaining Roosevelt's vision and commitment on behalf of the United States. On 26 June 1945 the Charter was unveiled at the city's Opera House and entered into formal force the following October. San Francisco in 1945 – after Westphalia in 1648, Vienna in 1815 and Versailles in 1919 – was the latest and still the most recent turn in the ever hopeful cycle of post-conflict regulation.

Homeless when the San Francisco event ended, the new organization did not have the most auspicious of beginnings. The General Assembly had to borrow Central Hall Westminster in London for its first session in January 1946 (when the League of Nations, long defunct in practice, ceased to exist as a legal entity). The UN's iconic modernist, thirty-eight storey headquarters building was eventually built on Manhattan's East River on land gifted by the Rockefeller family. Its location in

Figure 2 The United Nations Headquarters Building, East River, New York (UN Photo by Mark Garten)

the United States was accepted readily enough by the membership, though Britain and France expressed doubts. To base the new organization in what was referred to as the new world was an important symbolic shift in the global political order which had hitherto been unquestioningly Eurocentric. In purely numerical terms, after all, twenty-three out of the fifty-one members of the UN at the end of 1945 were from the Americas. As events turned out, within a few years the location of the world organization in New York would probably have been unthinkable. Whatever the virtues in moving the new organization's base from old Europe, to move it to the largest city in the United States would, after the arrival of the Cold War, have been regarded by the Soviet Union as a boost to the prestige of its ideological rival which had to be resisted.

2

Powers, bureaucracy and leadership

The founding document and basic constitution of the United Nations is the Charter which opened for signature at San Francisco in 1945.[4] It has 111 articles organized in nineteen chapters. Those who sign it, in other words the member states of the UN, become bound under international law to comply with its terms. Obligations under the Charter take precedence over all other international legal commitments that a signatory state may have entered into.

The Charter: what the UN can do

Chapters III to V and XV of the Charter deal with the composition and powers of the main bodies of the organization: the General Assembly, the Security Council and the Secretariat. Most of the remainder of the document is concerned with the powers and responsibilities of the UN as an international actor. Chapters VI, VII and VIII are central to the ultimate objective of the UN: peace and security. The range of the UN's social and economic responsibilities for global well-being, which has grown dramatically over the years, is covered in Chapters IX and X. Issues related to colonial trusteeship and non-self-governing territories – which declined in prominence more or less in step with the growth of international development issues – are dealt with in Chapters XI to XIII. Finally, the scope and powers of the International Court of Justice are outlined in Chapter XIV.

> ## THE PRINCIPAL ORGANS OF THE UNITED NATIONS
>
> General Assembly (Charter Chapter IV)
> Security Council (Charter Chapter V)
> Economic and Social Council (Charter Chapter X)
> Trusteeship Council (Charter Chapter XIII)
> International Court of Justice (Charter Chapter XIV)
> Secretariat (Charter Chapter XV)

Each of these issue areas will be explored in future chapters, but it is important to begin with an awareness of the basic purposes of the UN. These were set out in 1945 at the beginning of the Charter (see textbox) and remain unchanged today. Inevitably, given the context of the UN's creation, these are dominated by the question of international peace and security. Article 1 of the Charter emphasizes the collective nature of the measures the UN would employ towards maintaining peace and security.

> ## ARTICLE 1 OF THE UNITED NATIONS CHARTER
>
> *The Purposes of the United Nations are:*
>
> 1. *To maintain international peace and security, and to that end: to take effective collective measures for the prevention and removal of threats to the peace, and for the suppression of acts of aggression or other breaches of the peace, and to bring about by peaceful means, and in conformity with the principles of justice and international law, adjustment or settlement of international disputes or situations which might lead to a breach of the peace;*

ARTICLE 1 OF THE UNITED NATIONS CHARTER (*cont.*)

2. *To develop friendly relations among nations based on respect for the principle of equal rights and self-determination of peoples, and to take other appropriate measures to strengthen universal peace;*
3. *To achieve international cooperation in solving international problems of an economic, social, cultural, or humanitarian character, and in promoting and encouraging respect for human rights and for fundamental freedoms for all without distinction as to race, sex, language, or religion; and*
4. *To be a centre for harmonizing the actions of nations in the attainment of these common ends.*

The second article deals with the obligations of membership. These, fundamentally, involve compliance with the terms of the Charter. But, importantly, as well as laying out the responsibilities of member states, this article also underlines what might be called the Westphalian nature of world politics. The UN, the article states, is 'based on the principle of the sovereign equality of all its Members'. Moreover, nothing 'contained in the present Charter shall authorize the United Nations to intervene in matters which are essentially within the domestic jurisdiction of any state'. The important point here is that the UN is ultimately an inter-governmental organization designed to provide a forum for cooperation among independent states. It is not a supranational body transcending the sovereignty of its members and determining their national policies. In this it can be contrasted with, for example, the European Union, which in principle at any rate has such supranational powers.

The one condition attached to this bow to national sovereignty in the Charter concerns arrangements for collective security which we will look at in some detail later, but even here, as we will see, the UN's powers have never really been used. This tension between the philosophies of intergovernmentalism on one side and supranationalism on the other has been at the root of many of the UN's biggest problems over the years. Just as in the case of the League of Nations, the shortcomings of sovereign member states in supporting the organization have been conveniently passed off, frequently by the errant states themselves, as the shortcomings of the organization itself. The UN is often seen by the public as an independent actor, even a kind of ineffective superpower, when in reality it can do no more than its member states, and especially the biggest ones, are willing to permit. And, even here, what it is permitted is restricted by the prohibition on involvement in the domestic politics of states.

The General Assembly of the United Nations is, in principle if not in fact, its senior body. It meets in Regular Session annually, usually between September and December (though it can continue into the following year). Its plenary meetings are chaired by a president elected for each annual session. The Assembly can also convene emergency and special sessions at any time. The opening of the annual session normally becomes a gathering of the world's foreign ministers and often heads of state and government as well. These national leaders frequently use the opening of the General Assembly as a platform for major national foreign policy pronouncements. All 192 members of the United Nations are represented by national missions to the General Assembly. These missions, which can vary in membership from two or three in the case of small microstates to dozens among the big powers, consist of full-time diplomats and civil servants who take instructions directly from their respective governments. In the early days of the League it was proposed that Assembly delegates should be prominent citizens of their respective countries, distinguished by their personal

Figure 3 The General Assembly Amphitheatre (UN Photo by Eskinder Debebe)

achievements and free to take independent positions on the issues under discussion. Governments however do not readily give up control of their national representatives in this way, and such idealism did not feature in the planning of the United Nations.

The General Assembly meets both in plenary – or full – session and in more specialized Main Committees. These deal with specific areas (see textbox) and report back to the plenary session. Each of these committees consists of representatives of the full membership. The Assembly determines its own agenda and can debate and vote on what it chooses. Its resolutions are passed by a simple majority except where the Assembly itself determines them to be of particular importance, when a two-thirds majority is required. Since the end of the Cold War, during which there was a tendency for East and West to adopt contrary voting positions virtually as a matter of principle, an increasing number of decisions have been reached by consensus. Crucially, though, decisions of the General Assembly (other than those dealing with internal UN matters) are not legally binding on members as those of the Security Council may be. The force of the Assembly's decisions is purely moral, based on the fact that they can be claimed to represent the will of the world community.

THE MAIN COMMITTEES OF THE GENERAL ASSEMBLY

First Committee: Disarmament and International Security Committee
Second Committee: Economic and Financial Committee
Third Committee: Social, Humanitarian and Cultural Committee
Fourth Committee: Special Political and Decolonization Committee
Fifth Committee: Administrative and Budgetary Committee
Sixth Committee: Legal Committee

The Security Council is required to report to the General Assembly annually. The Assembly however is not permitted to deliberate on issues currently before the Council without being invited to do so by the Council. The General Assembly has a key role in appointments to the other principal organs of the UN, including the members of the Economic and Social Council. It also selects the non-permanent members of the Security Council. One of its greatest powers, at least in theory, lies in its responsibility for the admission of new members. It can exercise this, though, only on the recommendation of the Security Council where the initial stage of the application process is subject to the veto. Similarly, it formally appoints the secretary-general of the UN, but again only on the recommendation of the Security Council. It has a similar role in the appointment of judges to the International Court of Justice. More significantly, though, it controls the budget of the entire UN system (currently in the region of US$20 billion annually) and sets the 'assessments' – the annual contributions – of each UN member. In reality, the power of the General Assembly in world politics has been very variable and, over the long term, has declined in relation to that of the Security Council.

CONTRIBUTIONS TO THE UN REGULAR BUDGET FROM THE PERMANENT MEMBERS OF THE SECURITY COUNCIL (2006)

Nation	Assessed Percentage	Amount in US Dollars
China	2.05	$35,036,460
France	6.03	$102,907,868
Russia	1.10	$18,772,580
United Kingdom	6.13	$104,563,268
United States	22.00	$423,464,855

Ultimately, this is just a reflection of the real political world. The General Assembly's democratic structures are impressive. It is the embodiment of the principle of sovereign equality with each member, regardless of its size, population or the power it projects in the world, entitled to the same number of delegates (five) and the same single vote. All members are represented on its six Main Committees, each of which is responsible for a key area of the UN's mission.

Yet however impressive this devotion to sovereign equality may be as a principle, it is a major distortion of the realities of the international system. As we have seen, during the planning of the United Nations one of the main worries of the Soviet

Union was the automatic Western majority within the organization. While the veto power in the Security Council could protect Soviet interests there, the General Assembly with its parliamentary structure was a major concern. To meet this Stalin sought to have all the USSR's individual republics admitted. This was received at the time with general derision in the West. An exasperated President Roosevelt threatened to demand the admission of each and every state in the USA in retaliation. In the event, a compromise was reached whereby the two largest Soviet republics, Ukraine and Belorussia, were given separate membership (both became independent sovereign states with the break-up of the Soviet Union in 1992 – Belorussia becoming Belarus). But was the Soviet position so unreasonable? There was a legitimate argument about whether a state of the size, population, resource base and military capacity of the USSR should have exactly the same power in the General Assembly as, say, Haiti which was another founder member in 1945. In other words, the idea of sovereign equality is perhaps not as equitable as it might first appear.

Soviet fears were evidently justified in the early years of the organization. The General Assembly with its built-in Western majority became a very useful tool for the United States and its allies in the Cold War. During the Korean War the Soviet veto in the Security Council restricted the actions of the West which were being pursued under the banner of the UN. But the Americans contrived, through the Uniting for Peace resolution, to have security matters deadlocked in the Security Council simply transferred to the General Assembly where the writ of the West automatically ran (see Chapter 3).

Later, however, the balance of power in the General Assembly began to shift. This was due to the influx of new Afro-Asian states which came to independence – and UN membership – in the great surge of decolonization in the late 1950s and early 1960s. In the five years after 1955 alone, forty countries joined the UN (sixteen of them in one month in 1960). These new members were not so much actively pro–Soviet as wary of its rivals given their recent history as imperial possessions of Western states. The Afro–Asian bloc, as it came to be called, was assertively non–aligned in its approach to world politics. New political and economic priorities arrived at the UN with these new members. North–South issues began to cut across the East–West ones which dominated the General Assembly's debates for the first fifteen or twenty years of its existence. The new issues, concerned with colonial freedom, anti-racism and economic justice, tended to bring the Afro-Asians into conflict more with the Western bloc than the Eastern. The automatic anti-Soviet majority in the General Assembly therefore started to unravel in the 1960s. Henceforward complaints about the distortions of the General Assembly's democratic structure and the unreasonableness of its resolutions tended to be heard more from Western delegations than those of the Soviet bloc.

THE GLOBAL SOUTH IN THE GENERAL ASSEMBLY

Date	Membership	African	Asian/Pacific
1945	51	3	11
1960	100	22	30
1980	150	51	40

Afro-Asian membership: 1945 = 27%; 1980 = 60%

The high point of the General Assembly's authority and influence in world politics probably came at the end of the 1960s and the beginning of the 1970s. After this the Assembly was increasingly overshadowed by the Security Council. By the first decade of the twenty-first century the deliberations of the General Assembly appear to have very little impact on the momentous and pressing issues of the day such as war and peace and are more focused on less directly strategic (though no less important) issues such as development, the environment and the internal processes of the UN itself. The reasons for this relative decline in political authority are complex. For one thing, the rather grandiose ambitions of the non-aligned group in areas such as economic development and global redistribution of wealth were never realized. The economic and political leverage of the states of the global South, which was freely exercised in the General Assembly in the 1960s, declined rather than strengthened as the twentieth century drew to a close. Increasingly, the big powers in the Security Council sought to order the world in their own interests and exclude others from the process. Then, the end of the Cold War and the disappearance of opposing blocs removed the competition between East and West for the approval of the non-aligned. Previously perhaps this rivalry had led the superpowers and their allies to give more attention to the views of the General Assembly than the realities of power justified.

Yet despite these very real limits on the power of the General Assembly and its overshadowing by the Security Council notwithstanding, it is still an important international actor. Its plethora of special committees and commissions, dealing with everything from disarmament to peacekeeping to Palestine, produce original and influential reports on a whole gamut of global concerns. The General Assembly's decisions may not be legally binding, but they do set international norms and expectations which have an effect on the way states behave in their relations with one another.

EMERGENCY SPECIAL SESSIONS OF THE GENERAL ASSEMBLY

First	1956	Suez crisis
Second	1956	Soviet invasion of Hungary
Third	1958	Lebanon–Jordan–Syria tensions
Fourth	1960	Congo crisis
Fifth	1967	Arab–Israeli War
Sixth	1980	Soviet Invasion of Afghanistan
Seventh	1980	Palestine
Eighth	1981	South Africa/Namibia
Ninth	1982	Israeli occupied territories
Tenth	1997	Israeli occupied territories

The realities of power: the Security Council

All this considered, though, the real political power of the United Nations lies with the fifteen-strong Security Council. The Charter gives it the 'primary responsibility for the maintenance of international peace and security' and the members of the General Assembly 'agree that in carrying out its duties under this responsibility the Security Council acts on their behalf'.

The Security Council was to be the sheriff's office for the world policemen who, in President's Roosevelt original vision, would be responsible for the new system of collective security after the Second World War. At the outset only three policemen seemed ready to come on duty. The United States, the Soviet Union and Britain were the only obvious big power victors in the war. France, largely on the basis of its historical standing as a great power, was also eventually included. The need to establish a truly global organization, however – or at least one which wasn't simply transatlantic in its focus – opened the way for the admission of China (which unlike France had been present during the early planning stages of the UN) to the inner circle in 1945, despite its enfeebled state and unresolved civil war.

What exactly 'China' meant in political terms would prove a running sore in the UN for the first quarter century of its existence, however. In 1945 the legally recognized government of China was still constituted by the Nationalists under Chiang Kai-shek. By 1949, however, Mao Zedong's Communists had pushed Chiang's forces out of mainland China and now controlled the state in mainland China from Beijing. Despite this, the United States insisted that China should still be represented at the UN by the remnants of the Nationalist regime which had now retreated to the island of what was then known as Formosa (modern-day Taiwan). Possession being nine-tenths of the law in the UN as elsewhere, any move to adjust the situation would simply have been vetoed by the US and its allies. As a result, the government of a tiny, off-shore microstate continued to occupy a permanent seat on the Security Council with all the associated powers, including the veto. It was an absurd situation which brought the whole UN idea into discredit. It was also one which exposed the limits of the power of the General Assembly in membership questions as it was powerless to alter the situation in the face of the American position in the Security Council. The situation was not corrected until 1971 and then only when a self-interested shift in American foreign policy towards Communist China allowed Beijing into the UN. This also brought the unceremonious expulsion of Taiwan not just from the Security Council but the entire UN system.

The power of the five permanent members is qualified only by the presence of ten non-permanent members on the Security Council. One of the most common arguments for fundamental reform of the Security Council (and by extension the UN system as a whole) is based, so to speak, on the permanence of these permanent members. This structure sets in concrete the distribution of world power which pertained in the mid-twentieth century. This cannot be right, it is argued, as no such configuration of power remains unchanged over seven decades. Strangely, though, it more or less has. The five permanent members of the Council, despite the ebb and flow of power in the world since 1945, have stayed pretty well at the top of the political, military and economic hierarchy of states. This may be the first point in world history that such a situation has been witnessed, and it is obviously fortuitous rather than the outcome of far-sighted planning in the mid-1940s. But these five countries first became, and then remained for a considerable time, the world's only nuclear powers. They are still those with the only realistic capacity to manage truly effective nuclear deterrence. Their economies are still among the most powerful in an increasingly globalized world, and their quasi-imperial influence beyond their own borders is considerable.

This is not to say that arguments for reform based on wider representation cannot be made. Japan, Germany, even the European Union have all been suggested as possible new permanent members. Similarly, countries such as Brazil, South Africa and India have been proposed as regional superpowers whose permanent membership of the Security Council would bring a fairer geographical spread (see Chapter 8). But serious proposals for Security Council reform rarely involve the removal of any existing permanent member from the apex of power

In the absence of such reform, the regions of the world have to be content with non-permanent representation. Originally there were only six of these seats in the Security Council but this was expanded to ten in a Charter amendment in 1965 to take account of the massive growth in UN membership over the previous decade. These non-permanent members of the Security Council are elected by the General Assembly from among its membership on a regional basis for two-year terms.

Figure 4 The Security Council in Session (UN Photo by Ryan Brown)

Five of the ten rotate each year in order to give some continuity to representation and to avoid the disjunction of a complete change every two years. The non-permanent members are selected on a loose continental basis with five from what was once the Afro-Asian bloc, two from Latin America, two from Western Europe and one from Eastern Europe.

The president of the Security Council, who chairs its sessions, is selected by rotation from all fifteen members on a monthly basis. Each member of the Security Council, permanent and non-permanent, has a single vote. Routine procedural decisions are taken by a minimum majority of nine of the fifteen members. On substantive political and security issues, however, a majority of nine can be overturned by a single veto by a permanent member. This remains one of the most controversial aspects of the entire UN project. How, critics ask, can we think in terms of the UN as the voice of the international community when such a fundamentally anti-democratic mechanism lies at the heart of it? Moreover, the very existence of the veto, even short of its actual use, it is argued, can constrain discussion and decision in the Council. Important resolutions may be diluted or initiatives abandoned altogether when the shadow of a potential veto looms on the horizon (this hidden effect is sometimes referred to as the 'pocket veto').

Against this, though, a strong case can be made for the necessity of veto power. The veto lies at the precise pivot point between collective action on one side and the real world of big power politics on the other. If decisions in the Security Council were to be taken on the basis of a majority vote there would be two consequences, one philosophical the other bluntly practical. First, the absence of the power of veto (which, it should be borne in mind, itself was an advance on the unanimity rule in the League of Nations) would simply be incompatible with the idea of an international system of sovereign states. Second, and following on from this, in such a system of sovereign states any attempt to impose majority decisions would be doomed to failure – and would probably bring about the collapse of the United Nations as a whole. Attempts to impose particular policies or forms of behaviour on the permanent members would simply end with those members packing their bags and leaving. This would assuredly have happened when the Soviet Union was isolated both internationally and in the UN itself in the first decade or so after the organization was established. The Uniting for Peace Resolution of 1950, which attempted to navigate round likely Soviet vetoes over Korea by passing deadlocked business to the General Assembly, sailed very close to destructive winds in this respect. In the event this process was used only sparingly (or to Soviet satisfaction, as in 1956 during the Suez crisis) and was soon left dormant. Terminal crisis might have ensued much more recently if US administrations which were fundamentally suspicious of the whole idea of the UN had been denied the power to veto moves they perceived as against American interests. In short, the veto may be the minimum price necessary to guarantee the credibility of the Security Council and the existence of the UN as a whole.

The pattern of veto use over the years provides a revealing overview of the state of international politics. Initially, the veto was the province of the Soviet Union. So freely did its delegation use it – eighty out of a total of eighty-three blocking votes were cast by the USSR in the first ten years of the UN – that Foreign Minister Molotov became known as Mr Veto. Except in very special circumstances, none of the other permanent members used its veto power in these early years. Soon though, the change in the composition of the UN brought about by the process of decolonization and the emergence of the Afro-Asian bloc gave rise to new priority areas. These were often pursued by a new type of non-permanent member of the Security Council brought centre-stage by this broader shift in UN politics. The veto now became much more of a Western weapon in UN politics. Up until 2007 the veto had been used 279 times in all but the distribution of its use among the permanent members changed dramatically from about the mid-1960s (see textbox). Since the end of the Cold War its use has dwindled. Between 1980 and 1989, the last decade of the Cold War, fifty-one vetoes were cast. In the following ten years from 1990 to 1999 there were only nine.

VETO USE IN THE SECURITY COUNCIL

	US	USSR/Russ.	Britain	France	China
1946–1965	0	106	3	4	1
1966–1985	46	13	21	11	2
1986–2007	54	4	8	3	3
Total	100	123	32	18	6

One of the reasons for this decline in the exercise of the veto is that its use has become more politically costly since the end of the Cold War. As long as the world was divided in two camps, deploying the veto could be justified as a legitimate attempt to meet the inbuilt ill-will and political manoeuvrings of the other side – whichever side it was. With the end of polarized world politics this no longer stood. Now states will use the veto or otherwise ignore the Security Council only when there is no wriggle room and national interests are closely engaged. Veto use, perhaps because it has become rare, tends to attract very unfavourable attention now. In a world where the strategic and ideological demands of Cold War politics no longer operate, veto use seems doubly anti-democratic.

In general the permanent members (or the P5 as they are now sometimes described) will do everything they can to seek compromise through informal negotiations or even by removing an issue from the Security Council altogether rather than push a contested resolution to a vote. In 2003 the United States and Britain tried up until the last moment to obtain Security Council approval for their invasion of Iraq. Only when it became absolutely clear that they would fail did they opt for unilateral action. Before this, frantic conversations took place with promises and threats deployed in an attempt to secure support. According to the former British cabinet minister, Clare Short, the American government even asked British espionage agencies to bug Secretary-General Kofi Annan to determine his position. Eventually it became evident that the crucial new resolution legitimizing the war would either be vetoed (possibly even by nominal ally France) or more likely would simply fail to achieve the necessary majority of nine. Even then, however, the United States and Britain felt constrained to justify their subsequent military action on the basis of a 'first' resolution passed by the Security Council in the aftermath of the earlier Gulf War in 1991. Four years earlier in 1999 the risk of failure in the

Security Council, possibly via a Russian veto, led Britain and the United States to prepare their action against Serbia over the Kosovo situation in the context of the North Atlantic Treaty Organization and later presented it as a fait accompli to the Security Council.

If an accommodation cannot be found, then abstentions are now much more likely than vetoes. The position of the United States in the final days of the Bush administration at the beginning of 2009 is telling here. In the face of worldwide criticism of Israel's military action in Gaza, the American delegation did not veto a critical Security Council resolution as it almost certainly would have done even a few years previously. The best Washington felt able to do for its Israeli allies, despite the natural inclination of President George W. Bush himself, was abstain in the vote. More and more, a veto has become a major political event and one to be avoided where at all possible.

Increasingly then, the Security Council has become a forum for cooperation rather than an arena of conflict. Its security responsibilities primarily involve the establishment and management of peacekeeping operations and humanitarian interventions often followed by oversight of post-conflict peace-building processes. Peacekeeping, which has grown enormously since the early 1990s, has always been a Security Council responsibility, but in the past it has been a highly contested one. During the Cold War the Soviet Union was instinctively suspicious of the concept of peacekeeping, often seeing it as a Western conspiracy (see Chapter 4). Arguments about peacekeeping now, in contrast, tend to be over the appropriate use of limited financial and manpower resources.

This is not to say that sweetness and light always prevails in the contemporary Security Council. The conflict around the Iraq issue in 2003 was intense and deeply felt. It exposed, to some degree, a cleavage which in ways pre-dated that of the East versus West rift of the Cold War. This was the transatlantic division evident when Woodrow Wilson pressed his idea for a League of Nations on his reluctant European allies and then failed to prevail against the isolationist instincts of his fellow American politicians. It was, at least to a degree, the same dividing line described by the American secretary of defence in 2003 at the time of the invasion, Donald Rumsfeld, as separating the 'old' from the 'new' Europe. (Few though would see the neoconservative Rumsfeld in a Wilsonian light.) Similarly, divisions in the Security Council over the Balkans also look back to long-standing historical affinities and hostilities. Russia's sympathies for Serbia, which determined the Anglo-American decision to keep the Kosovo issue away from the Security Council for as long as possible, are rooted in pan-Slavic sentiments. These affinities date at least from the nineteenth century and therefore long pre-date the Cold War. But by any measure, the Security Council of the early twenty-first century is a profoundly different political place from the Security Council of the mid-twentieth century.

Administration: the Secretariat

The Secretariat of the United Nations consists of the considerable body of officials necessary to run the organization. It numbers about 9000 permanent staff at the various headquarters buildings – which has been reduced from a high of around 11,000 in the 1990s. The cull followed pressure, mainly from the United States, for a leaner and fitter bureaucracy. At any one time, though, the Secretariat as a whole, including temporary appointments and officers in the field, amounts to around 30,000. Like so much else in the construction of the UN, the Secretariat was originally modelled very closely on its forerunner in the League of Nations. In principle the loyalty of its members lies with the institution and not with their countries of citizenship or their governments. As the Charter puts it, in 'the performance of their duties the ... staff shall not seek or receive instructions from any government or from any other authority external to the Organization. They shall refrain from any action which might reflect on their position as international officials responsible only to the Organization' (Chapter XV, article 100).

The Secretariat is led by a secretary-general who himself (and it always has been 'him' since the establishment of the UN) is a figure of considerable political influence and power within the organization. In 1998 a new position of deputy secretary-general was created. Below this there is a stratum of under-secretaries-general, each with a specific area of responsibility (such as peace-keeping, economic and social affairs, and humanitarian affairs). The permanent staff of the Secretariat is located across the UN's various centres, mainly in New York, Geneva (at the old Palais des Nations of the League), Vienna and Nairobi.

While as vulnerable as any large organization to bureaucratic politics and rivalries, over the life of the UN the Secretariat has developed a distinct group identity. Its essential blend of ideal-ism and professionalism was recognized by the award of the 2001 Nobel Peace Prize to the organization. Talk of the United Nations family is more than just self-regarding rhetoric. Its tight group identity was in evidence for example following the killing in a car bomb attack of the secretary-general's representative in Iraq in 2003, Sérgio Vieira de Melo. The Brazilian Viera de Melo was a quintessential UN animal, having been a member of the Secretariat for thirty-four years at the time of his death. During his career he held such senior posts as administrator of East Timor and High Commissioner for Refugees. The deeply felt reaction of fellow members of the UN bureaucracy to this death in action, so to speak, crystallized the powerful sense of mission within the Secretariat.

Despite this strong sense of purpose, the composition and conduct of the Secretariat has often been a focus for critics of the

United Nations. Too many senior positions, they argue, are filled on the basis of national quotas rather than on merit and ability. It is certainly true that governments will use their ability to appoint individuals to high status and financially lucrative UN posts as a form of political patronage. Occasionally too, such appointments will be used as a means of quietly solving the problem of political figures who have become inconvenient or embarrassing to governments. As a result, accusations of incompetence and corruption are not unusual. Sometimes, however, this has as much to do with political disagreement as personal conduct. In the 1980s, for example, considerable attention was focused on the conduct of the director-general of the UN Educational, Scientific and Cultural Organization (UNESCO), Amadou M'Bow of Senegal. M'Bow was accused of extravagance, grandiosity and mismanagement by the right-wing governments of the time in the United States and Britain. There was almost certainly some truth in the accusations, but perhaps M'Bow's main crime lay in what was perceived as the anti-Western bias of UNESCO under his direction. The affair grew into a crisis when both the US and Britain withdrew from the organization, returning only after considerable reform within UNESCO and changes of government in both Washington and London.

Bureaucrats or statesmen? The secretaries-general

Major global actors in their own right, the eight secretaries-general who have held office since the formation of the UN have been at the centre of the major world events of their times and have frequently shaped them. The prescribed term of office is five years, though most secretaries-general have been appointed for a second term. The Charter itself gives the secretary-general an important power of personal initiative. Although article 97 of the Charter describes the post simply as 'the chief administrative officer of the Organization', article 99 empowers him to 'bring to the attention of the Security Council any matter which in his opinion may threaten the maintenance of international peace and security'. This is a prerogative which has been used sparingly but incisively over the years.

Although nominally appointed by the General Assembly, the real selection process for the secretary-general takes place among the five permanent members of the Security Council. Their deliberations, always protracted and intense, and the consensus that emerges from them, have not always produced the safe pair of hands predicted. Several secretaries-general, whether on their own initiative or by simple circumstances, have found themselves in serious conflict with one, or more, permanent member of the Security Council. A short account of the politics and personalities of each of the secretaries-general to date provides a thumbnail sketch of the shifting preoccupations of the organization itself.

Trygve Lie (1946–1953) The UN's first secretary-general was the Norwegian, Trygve Lie. At the time of his appointment at the beginning of 1946 he was a compromise choice in a wrangle which portended problems to come. The favoured candidate of the United States was the Canadian foreign minister, Lester Pearson. He was rejected by the Soviet Union as too Western. The Soviet proposal of the Yugoslav foreign minister was almost a mirror image from the Communist side and was, unsurprisingly, rejected by the Americans. Trygve Lie seemed to offer a relatively uncontroversial neutral choice. A lawyer by profession, he was prominent in centre-left politics in Norway and had been foreign minister in the Norwegian government in exile during the Nazi occupation in the Second World War. If anything, he was more favoured by the Soviet Union than the

West at the outset. His term of office coincided with some early challenges to the UN, including the formation of the state of Israel in the former Palestine mandate, and the conflicts following the independence of India and Pakistan. In each of these crises he oversaw the first tentative moves towards what would later become peacekeeping. He was also an early – though unsuccessful – advocate for the admission of Communist China to the organization.

His position in the politics of the UN changed dramatically in 1950 with the outbreak of the Korean War, however. His support for the American-led, though nominally UN intervention against North Korea provoked the implacable hostility of the Soviet Union. His position was somewhat compromised too when Norway became a founding member of NATO in 1949. If the ire of the Soviet Union was not enough of a burden, he also drew fire from the anti-Communist witch-hunters influential in the American administration at the time. In their world the UN was a hopeless left-liberal organization and its chief executive became an important target of anti-red righteousness. His term was extended in 1950 but he did not serve out the full five years. He retired in 1953 leaving a UN in crisis as the Cold War began to freeze its activities.

Dag Hammarskjöld (1953–1961) Lie was succeeded by his fellow Scandinavian, Dag Hammarskjöld. Son of a First World War Swedish prime minister, he was brought up at the centre of the country's political elite. His early career had been as a successful but unspectacular civil servant and he seemed to offer the quietly competent temperament that the UN, badly damaged by the Korean conflict and Cold War issues in general, seemed to need. Sweden's traditional neutrality was also a useful factor in his appointment. Once in office, however, Hammarskjöld proved to be much more of a visionary and activist than had been expected. His time at the head of the UN was one in which huge stresses were being exerted on the international system by the intertwined phenomena of decolonization and Cold War. In his first five year term he was particularly involved in the Middle East and in 1956 was instrumental in the creation of the UN's first large-scale peacekeeping operation after the Anglo-French invasion of Suez. His second term, following his reappointment in 1957, became dominated by Africa, then becoming the main focus of decolonization. In 1960 he urged the creation of another major peacekeeping effort, this time in the Congo amid the chaos following Belgium's rapid and inadequately planned withdrawal.

In some respects the Congo was to be for Hammarskjöld what Korea had been for his predecessor, though with a much more tragic personal outcome. The crisis was quickly sucked into the broader Cold War contest and Hammarskjöld was denounced by the Soviet Union as a pro-Western stooge. Hammarskjöld's so-called Congo Club of Secretariat advisers was indeed exclusively Western in composition and there was some evidence that Eastern bloc officials had been deliberately excluded. This might have made practical sense as the principle of institutional rather than national loyalty was not always applied by Eastern bloc members of the Secretariat. But it was politically toxic. By 1961 the affair had grown into a major crisis for the United Nations system as a whole. The Soviet leader Nikita Khrushchev now angrily demanded nothing less than the abolition of the office of secretary-general on the basis that there were neutral countries but no neutral men. The Secretariat, he argued, should be placed under a 'troika' (or trio) of individuals, one nominated by the Western bloc, one by Communist Eastern Europe and one by the emerging Afro-Asian group. The plan was not in the event adopted by the General Assembly. Had it been so, though, it would have signalled the end of the UN's ambition to be a cooperative global organization. It would have consolidated rather than confronted the divisions of the international system of the time. But the UN was greatly damaged by the affair.

In September 1961, a few months after the troika plan had been debated in New York, Hammarskjöld was killed when his aircraft crashed in Northern Rhodesia as he flew to emergency talks with one of the Congolese factions. Shortly afterwards he was posthumously awarded the Nobel Peace Prize. Hammarskjöld and his legacy have attracted more discussion probably than all the other secretaries-general put together. A complex, often rather tortured individual, he wrote bleak, highly personal poetry during his UN career which was published posthumously. He was certainly a long way from being the dull public servant that the Security Council thought it was appointing in 1953. Unquestionably, his death ended one of the most significant periods in the development of the UN.

U Thant (1961–1971) Immediately following Hammarskjöld's death U Thant of Burma was named as acting secretary-general (the term 'U' is a general honorific in Burma, Thant was his single name). Thant was originally a rather obscure compromise candidate brought in to break the deadlock in a deeply divided Security Council. Yet this was a significant appointment in its implicit acknowledgement of the importance in the UN of what would soon be known as the Third World. A schoolteacher for many years before entering government service after Burma's independence in 1948, Thant had been the country's permanent delegate to the UN at the time of Hammarskjöld's death. In the event, he turned out to be just the calming influence that the organization needed at a particularly febrile time in both UN and world politics. A practicing Buddhist, Thant brought the contemplative style of his religion to his office.

In November 1962 his position was regularized when he was appointed to serve a full term as substantive secretary-general. It is possible that this outcome owed something to his quiet and even-handed diplomacy during the Cuban missile crisis of the previous month. He was reappointed for a second term in 1966. Thant presided over a period of enormous growth in the UN, not only in membership but in the range of the organization's activities as well. Perhaps his greatest achievement, however, lay in quietly steering the UN through one of the most dangerous periods in post-1945 world history and leaving it in much greater health than he had found it. As well as the Cuban crisis, his term in office, which ended in 1971, encompassed the main surge of decolonization, the 1967 Six Day War in the Middle East, the Soviet invasion of Czechoslovakia in 1968 and, perhaps most significantly, the Vietnam War. His opposition to the last affected his relations with Washington for a time, but he was the first UN secretary-general to leave office as well regarded by both East and West as he had been when first appointed. So high was his credit at the end that he had to resist pressure to stand for an unprecedented third term. When Thant died in 1974 after a long illness his funeral became the occasion of widespread demonstrations against Burma's military rulers.

Kurt Waldheim (1972–1981) The two Security Council superpowers found great difficulty in reaching agreement over Thant's successor. Eventually, they retreated to the safe resort of a traditional European neutral. The Austrian Kurt Waldheim appeared to be a reliable, conventional figure. A career diplomat in post-war Austria, he had been part of the country's first delegation to the UN. Later, between 1968 and 1970, he served as Austria's foreign minister, after which he became Austrian permanent representative at the United Nations. His appointment as UN secretary-general followed an unsuccessful campaign for the Austrian presidency as candidate for the centre-right Peoples Party. As secretary-general Waldheim proved to be a competent if rather unadventurous administrator. He was, however, somewhat notorious among his staff for his grand manner and highly developed sense of his own importance. In 1976 he was reappointed for the now customary second term, though only after some tense debate in the Security Council.

Waldheim's term in office coincided with the period of relaxation in tensions between the superpowers which came to be known as détente. This meant that he was spared many of the more intractable difficulties involved in balancing competing Cold War interests and demands which other secretaries-general had to manage. He faced some criticism, however, for apparently placing the United Nations at the disposal of superpower interests and the neglect of those of its less powerful members. Waldheim sought a third term in office at the end of 1981 but this was vetoed by Communist China which resented his closeness to the United States and the Soviet Union.

In 1986 Waldheim realized his earlier ambitions by being elected president of Austria. His achievement was overshadowed, at least abroad, by revelations during the campaign that he had covered up a controversial period of service with the German army in the Balkans during the Second World War. This led to his being banned from entering the United States, a prohibition which remained in place until his death in 2007.

Javier Pérez de Cuéllar (1982–1991) The fifth secretary-general of the UN was the first from the Western hemisphere, Javier Pérez de Cuéllar of Peru. His two terms, from 1982 to 1991, embraced both the most intense phase of the post-détente 'second' Cold War and the final end of the divided world order. Pérez de Cuéllar was a career civil servant whose work for the Peruvian foreign ministry had intermittently involved him with the United Nations. As a junior diplomat in 1946 he had been part of his country's delegation to the first UN General Assembly in Central Hall Westminster. After leading the Peruvian delegation in New York during the 1970s, he was appointed UN under-secretary-general for Political Affairs in which capacity he was engaged in attempts to resolve the conflict in Afghanistan following the Soviet invasion of 1978. His two major achievements as secretary-general were the negotiation of the end of the Iran–Iraq war in 1988 and

Namibia's transition to independence from South Africa in 1989–1990. Less successfully, he sought to negotiate a compromise between Britain and Argentina over the Falklands in 1982 and to resolve the complex of civil conflicts between left-wing insurgents and US-supported rightist regimes in Central America in the 1980s.

Paradoxically but perhaps inevitably, his role in the momentous world events of the late 1980s which saw the end of the Cold War was limited. This was an era in which the superpowers still closely guarded their own policy initiatives; it was not a time for the UN's brand of intergovernmentalism. Pérez de Cuéllar did however preside over the UN's legitimization of the first Gulf War in 1991 which followed Iraq's invasion of Kuwait, the first major post-Cold War international conflict. The very end of his time in office marked the beginning of a new phase of UN activism. The consequences, positive and negative, of the end of the Cold War increasingly demanded multilateral solutions and the UN was called on to provide them. Like Kurt Waldheim his predecessor, Pérez de Cuéllar sought to pursue a national political career after retiring from the UN. Unlike Waldheim, however, he failed in a presidential bid in 1995. He did, however, at the age of eighty, serve as Peruvian foreign minister for a short time in 2000 and 2001.

Boutros Boutros-Ghali (1992–1996) Pérez de Cuéllar was succeeded by another figure from what could loosely be described as the South, Egypt's Boutros Boutros-Ghali. The UN's first wholly post-Cold War secretary-general would prove to be an altogether more controversial figure than his predecessor, however. This was not foreseen at the time of his appointment. He appeared to be a somewhat withdrawn and colourless figure – a view which chimed with his background as an academic and international lawyer. Born into a patrician Coptic Christian family, Boutros-Ghali was part of the Westernized elite which surrounded President Anwar Sadat in whose administration he first held political office. He eventually rose to the position of deputy foreign minister and then, in 1991, deputy prime minister of Egypt. His appointment to the post of secretary-general was seen as a clever compromise which gave the UN a Third World leader, but one who would not cause any radical ripples. In fact he proved to be something of an activist, with a personal mission to reform the UN to equip it to meet the new challenges and seize the new opportunities of the post-Cold War world. He was particularly interested in the peacekeeping function of the organization. It was ironic therefore that he was destined to preside over some of its greatest failures in Bosnia, Somalia and Rwanda.

Towards the end of what would normally have been his first term in office he found himself increasingly at odds with the Clinton administration in Washington. Friction emerged from his exasperation with American inconsistency over the UN's peacekeeping role (from its initial gung-ho approach in Somalia to evasion over Rwanda). But Boutros-Ghali also became unpopular with the ever-powerful Israel lobby in Washington as he pressed for a more robust and even-handed approach to the multiple problems of the Middle East. In 1996, despite strong support from other members of the Security Council, the United States vetoed his second term. In 1999 he published his own account of the conflict in his memoir, *Unvanquished: a US–UN Saga*. Boutros-Ghali has been the only secretary-general thus far not to have been reappointed.

Kofi Annan (1997–2006) The United States was much happier with Boutros-Ghali's successor, at least at the outset. Kofi Annan, from Ghana, was a highly experienced African diplomat who could, it was felt, be relied upon to bring the steadiness to the management of the organization promised but not delivered by his predecessor. Prior to taking over the top post Annan had been under-secretary-general for peacekeeping, a position he had reached after a lifelong career in international organizations. This career had not been without controversy. As head of peacekeeping during the Rwanda genocide of 1994 he was criticized by many, including the UN force commander on the ground, for a lack of engagement and urgency in the face of the crisis. His first term in office passed off without great drama though much of it was taken up in attempts to cut costs and increase efficiency in the Secretariat. This potentially divisive process was eased by his insider status and the genuine affection in which he was held by colleagues.

Soon after his reappointment to a second term was confirmed by the Security Council in 2002, however, the international climate and Annan's own position changed dramatically. The invasion of Iraq in March 2003 by the United States and Britain in the absence of clear United Nations authorization placed Annan in an impossibly difficult situation. He could either condemn the action in the interests of the rule of international law and the authority of the UN or he could retain his good relationship and influence with the two permanent Security Council members by remaining silent. For some time he sought by diplomatic sleight of hand to stay detached from the question of the legality of the war. Eventually in 2004, in palpable discomfort, he stated that the invasion, 'from our point of view, from the Charter point of view ... was illegal'.[5]

Annan's once strong relationship with the United States now deteriorated. His position was not helped by a number of scandals over the alleged involvement of family members in irregular dealings connected with the Iraq sanctions regime prior to the invasion. At one point there seemed to be a serious prospect of his resignation. He survived the furore, however, and left office with his integrity damaged but not destroyed at the end of 2006. He immediately became part of the senior branch of the global great and good and has been involved in a number of charitable activities, many of them related to African development.

Ban Ki-moon (2007–) The post-Annan succession saw the post go to an Asian for the first time since U Thant. The pressure for some gesture to regional equity was probably a real consideration for Security Council members when they appointed Ban Ki-moon of South Korea. His nationality was significant given the long and fraught history between the UN and the Korean peninsula, dating back to the war of 1950–1953. His appointment at an earlier phase in this history would have been unthinkable because of South Korea's close alignment with the West and impossible anyway, as South Korea was not even a member of the UN until 1991. Ban came as a complete contrast to his predecessor. Annan had been perceived as emotional, warm and approachable, while Ban appeared a somewhat bland and colourless bureaucrat. But the upside of this contrast was that Ban exuded administrative competence while Annan had often appeared reluctant to confront difficult managerial issues. Ban's appointment was certainly welcomed by the West. A career diplomat, he had been a postgraduate student at Harvard in the 1980s at a time when the relationship between the United States and South Korea had been extremely close. He had – perhaps more by hard work and diligence than sparkling talent – become South Korea's foreign minister, a position he held for most of the three years prior to taking up the UN appointment. In this post he had been supportive of American policy in Iraq (in fact had urged Korean involvement in the occupation). Although something of an outside bet at the beginning of the race to become the UN's eighth secretary-general, he had proved an assiduous campaigner and, probably most importantly, was the candidate who drew least opposition from any one part of the Security Council.

On taking office Ban quickly began a process of managerial reform. His own actions within the politics of the UN, however, have caused some controversy. While rightly applauded for promoting more women to the higher offices in the Secretariat, his tendency to place Western diplomats in the key under-secretary-general posts has caused misgivings. But at a time when one of the major challenges facing the UN is the effective (re) attachment of the United States to multilateral diplomacy, this partiality may be the necessary price to be paid. His evident capacity to plan and implement radical managerial change also endeared him to American foreign policy sceptics.

This, then, is the superstructure within which the United Nations operates. It is one which has been subject to questioning and criticism more or less since it was first constructed in 1945. Yet it has endured remarkably unchanged in its main outlines, partly it must be said through a combination of bureaucratic inertia and the natural tendency of those with power to fight to maintain it. But it would be wrong to neglect the fact that it has lasted too because it seems to work.

3
Peace I: Collective security and arms control

In keeping with its wartime origins, conflict and peace have always been at the centre of the UN's concerns. The first words of the preamble to the Charter pronounces this overarching priority (see textbox). The founding aspiration of the United Nations was for a truly collective system of global security and in a sense everything else – international development, humanitarianism, the rule of law – is secondary to this larger aim. After all, these objectives can only be properly achieved in a stable, secure and peaceful global environment.

Collective security as law

Roosevelt's founding idea was that explicit legal obligation – which had been absent from the League of Nations – was the main route to an effective system of collective security and this pervaded the construction of the UN. In this view the failure of collective security in the 1930s was not due to the extreme tensions of the time nor the underlying nature of a system based on sovereign statehood. It was simply that the League did not demand enough in sufficiently robust formal terms. This latest attempt at post-war regulation therefore would involve transparent and inescapable obligations under international law. In

PREAMBLE TO THE CHARTER OF THE UNITED NATIONS

WE THE PEOPLES OF THE UNITED NATIONS DETERMINED

to save succeeding generations from the scourge of war, which twice in our lifetime has brought untold sorrow to mankind, and

to reaffirm faith in fundamental human rights, in the dignity and worth of the human person, in the equal rights of men and women and of nations large and small, and

to establish conditions under which justice and respect for the obligations arising from treaties and other sources of international law can be maintained, and to promote social progress and better standards of life in larger freedom,

AND FOR THESE ENDS

to practice tolerance and live together in peace with one another as good neighbors, and

to unite our strength to maintain international peace and security, and

to ensure by the acceptance of principles and the institution of methods, that armed force shall not be used, save in the common interest, and

to employ international machinery for the promotion of the economic and social advancement of all peoples,

HAVE RESOLVED TO COMBINE OUR EFFORTS TO ACCOMPLISH THESE AIMS

Accordingly, our respective Governments, through representatives assembled in the city of San Francisco, who have exhibited their full powers found to be in good and due form, have agreed to the present Charter of the United Nations and do hereby establish an international organization to be known as the United Nations.

important respects, the evolution of the United Nations from this idealistic starting point illustrates the mismatch between visionary schemes and the realities of power politics in a particularly dangerous age. The obligations of the Charter remain unchanged since 1945 but the intervening decades have seen the most creative efforts by member states to navigate round them or, on occasion, to bend them to their own national ends.

The central statement of the UN's ambitions to create a truly new post-war world order is located in Chapter VII (articles 39–51) of the Charter, 'Action with Respect to Threats to the Peace, Breaches of the Peace and Acts of Aggression'. Article 39 gives the Security Council the power to determine the existence of any such dangers to global peace. The Council is then required to 'decide what measures shall be taken ... to maintain or restore' peace and security. Articles 41 and 42 list the options available to the UN if an aggressive state fails to comply with an order to desist. They begin with actions which fall short of military force, including economic sanctions, transport and communications blockades and the suspension of diplomatic relations between UN members and the aggressor. But if these measures are inadequate article 42 empowers the Security Council to 'consider ... such action by air, sea, or land forces as may be necessary'. To this end article 43 requires that all UN members 'undertake to make available to the Security Council, on its call ... armed forces, assistance and facilities'.

During the planning of the Charter the idea was mooted of a standing army whose members would have the same institutional loyalty as the Secretariat. Had the plan been pursued, of course, article 43 would have been unnecessary. National contributions to the UN's capacity for force would have been made up front, so to speak. A permanent UN force based on levies among its members would simply have been sent into action when required. The idea was not developed, mainly because it was considered wasteful to have a permanent force employed to meet only occasional extreme situations. Interestingly, in this pre-Cold War phase, the idea of a permanent UN army was not thought of as politically unworkable in itself. In the absence of such a permanent army, however, UN forces were to be created as circumstances demanded from among the member states. These would be placed under a command structure directed by the chiefs of staff of the

THE ENFORCEMENT POWERS OF THE SECURITY COUNCIL FROM CHAPTER VII OF THE CHARTER

Article 41

The Security Council may decide what measures not involving the use of armed force are to be employed to give effect to its decisions, and it may call upon the Members of the United Nations to apply such measures. These may include complete or partial interruption of economic relations and of rail, sea, air, postal, telegraphic, radio, and other means of communication, and the severance of diplomatic relations.

Article 42

Should the Security Council consider that measures provided for in Article 41 would be inadequate or have proved to be inadequate, it may take such action by air, sea, or land forces as may be necessary to maintain or restore international peace and security. Such action may include demonstrations, blockade, and other operations by air, sea, or land forces of Members of the United Nations.

Article 43

1. All Members of the United Nations, in order to contribute to the maintenance of international peace and security, undertake to make available to the Security Council, on its call and in accordance with a special agreement or agreements, armed forces, assistance, and facilities, including rights of passage, necessary for the purpose of maintaining international peace and security.

permanent members of the Security Council – the embodiment of Roosevelt's five policemen. This Military Staff Committee (MSC) is dealt with in article 47 of the Charter. The five senior generals, one from each of the P5, are 'responsible under the Security Council for the strategic direction of any armed forces placed at the disposal of the Security Council'.

The potential demands on UN members are therefore extremely burdensome. The Charter requires (it does not 'request') sovereign states to place their military forces under t he command of foreign generals and to fight in conflicts, however distant, dangerous or controversial, on the orders of the five permanent members of the Security Council. What is remarkable is how these requirements had such little impact on countries' calculations about UN membership. Admittedly, a few years into the life of the UN it was already clear that Chapter VII, or at least article 43, would probably never be properly invoked. But in 1945 it was a very real commitment. At that time only Switzerland held back. Despite being virtually the personification of the good global citizen – the founding nation of the international Red Cross and permanent host to the League of Nations – Switzerland regarded UN membership as incompatible with its constitutional commitment to neutrality. Chapter VII of the Charter made the UN, in the Swiss view, a military alliance. Only in 2002, with the Cold War long past and article 43 never having been summoned into action, did Switzerland overcome its constitutional scruples and enter the UN.

The last part of Chapter VII, article 51 of the Charter, has been presented from time to time as a national escape clause from the collective security project and a pragmatic recognition of the persisting power of the sovereign state system. It recognizes the 'inherent right of individual or collective self-defence'. At the time of the invasion of Iraq some international lawyers tried, rather tentatively, to use article 51 to justify the

US-led military action in the absence of a clear legitimizing
resolution of the Security Council. Their argument was based
on the notion that self-defence could be pre-emptive. Because
Iraq possessed weapons of mass destruction and the means to
deliver them (or so it was claimed at the outset of the invasion),
the United States and Britain were legally justified in taking
military action. Even putting aside the fact that no such weapons
existed, it was an unconvincing legal argument. Article 51
covers emergency situations in which a surprise attack can be
resisted only 'until the Security Council has taken measures
necessary to maintain international peace and security'. Self-
defence was never meant to provide a unilateral alternative to
collective security; it was a possible preliminary to collective
action in extreme situations, but no more than that.

The 'Regional Arrangements' for security which are set out
in Chapter VIII of the Charter have also been seen as a means
of evading commitment to global collective security. The

KOFI ANNAN ON THE DILEMMAS OF FORCE IN CONTEMPORARY INTERNATIONAL RELATIONS (FROM 'UN MEMBERS AND THE USE OF FORCE', 2005)

'an essential part of the consensus we seek must be agreement on
when and how force can be used to defend international peace
and security. In recent years, this issue has deeply divided Member
States. They have disagreed about whether States have the right to
use military force pre-emptively, to defend themselves against
imminent threats; whether they have the right to use it preven-
tively to defend themselves against latent or non-imminent
threats; and whether they have the right — or perhaps the obligation — to use it protectively to rescue the citizens of other States
from genocide or comparable crimes.'

apparent legitimacy given here to local military alliances might seem to cut across the central role of the UN in international security. But Chapter VIII makes clear that regional security groupings may exist only if they 'and their activities are consistent with the Purposes and Principles of the United Nations'. The Security Council, according to article 53, could use regional bodies as part of its collective security powers, but they could act only 'under its authority'. Security measures could be franchised by the UN to local alliances, therefore, but they could not be snatched away from it. The North Atlantic Treaty which brought NATO into being in 1949 is at pains to emphasize its legally subordinate role in this respect and is peppered with references to the United Nations and its powers.

The dominance of the permanent members of the Security Council that was central to the plan for UN collective security was not accepted without some reluctance by the smaller powers. When the final touches were being put to the plans at San Francisco some of the more self-confident second rank countries argued that the arrangements were undemocratic and out of step with the principle of sovereign equality. Australia and New Zealand in particular tried to expand the role of the General Assembly into the security area. Specifically, their plan would have given the Assembly the right to approve any military enforcement action proposed by the Security Council. But this would have undermined a fundamental prop of the whole project – the concentration of responsibility on those best able to exercise it – and it was rejected by the permanent members-in-waiting of the Security Council.

This was hardly surprising. Governments are as resistant to surrendering their special powers in the international system just as much as they are in their own countries. The fundamental problem for the UN's ambitions, however, was that this collective desire by the permanent members to keep power concentrated in their own hands was not matched by a collective view of the world. It might just have been argued in 1945 that this need not be the case. The big powers had, after all, just won a war as interdependent allies. They had welded themselves into an effective unified force (the original 'United Nations') against a group of common enemies. But negative signs were gathering even as the Charter was signed. The arguments over membership and the veto power and the wrangles over the appointment of the first secretary-general were all portents of what was rapidly developing into a Cold War in a polarized world.

Collectivity and polarization are, quite simply, wholly opposed concepts and it was the second that came to dominate the terms of international relations in the UN and outside it. The Charter itself did not do anything to ease the difficulties which flowed from this situation. The word 'aggression' is used throughout it, but nowhere is it actually defined. In a divided world, conflict is always seen through fundamentally different lenses. The view through one of these lenses might expose a blatant and shameless act of aggression; through another the view might as readily be of a justifiable and legitimate act of self-defence. In a polarized world, in other words, aggressors and victims will be identified according to political preference and not by undefined legal description. Without even a minimal level of consensus the grandiose plans of the Charter began to look faintly ludicrous.

Exposing the limits of collective security: the Korean War

Clear proof of the fragility of the ambitions of the Charter came in June 1950 when North Korea invaded South Korea. After the expulsion of Japan from the Korean peninsula these two de facto states had emerged under their respective allied occupiers: the Soviet Union in the North and the United States in the South (a situation roughly comparable to that in Germany at the same time). Korea provided a sharp illustration of the two lenses approach to defining aggression in a polarized world. The Western lens showed a clear and unambiguous act of international aggression of exactly the sort that the United Nations existed to confront. The Communist lens in contrast showed a legitimate attempt to bring about the unification of Korea agreed by all the allies at the end of the war but reneged on by the South and its Western supporters.

Quite by chance, the Soviet Union was boycotting the Security Council at the time of the invasion (in protest against the refusal of the Western powers to admit Communist China to the UN). The inevitable veto on UN action against North Korea was not, therefore, delivered and the Security Council could denounce the invasion, using the language of Chapter VII, as a breach of the peace. Article 43, which would have required UN members to provide the means to enforce the Security Council's will, was not invoked however. The Military Staff Committee could not have been properly convened without the Soviet Union, and anyway Moscow's boycott of the Security Council would obviously not continue in the new circumstances. Nevertheless, the Council 'recommended' that UN members 'furnish such assistance to the Republic of Korea as may be necessary to repel the armed attack and restore international peace and security in the area'.[6] This took the form of a so-called Unified Command of what were self-described as 'United Nations' forces. In reality this was an American-led coalition which occupied legal ground far distant from Chapter VII of the Charter. Two-thirds of the forces involved were provided by the United States and the other third came from its NATO allies and other friends in the Asia-Pacific region. American generals, not the Military Staff Committee, planned and directed the war.

The conflict dragged on for three years with advances and retreats by both sides across the thirty-eighth parallel (or line of latitude) which divided the two parts of the Korean peninsula. Along the way, Communist Chinese forces were thrown in to support North Korea and loose talk by American commanders about the use of nuclear weapons sent a chill through the world. Eventually, in 1953 an armistice was agreed along the original border, though hostilities have never been formally concluded up to the present.

Korea thoroughly skewered any claim the UN may have had to possessing enforceable means of collective security. Worse, after the creation of the Unified Command, the organization was coming to look suspiciously like just another Western alliance. Was the UN now doomed to follow the League into obscurity? Or could it find a new route to relevance in its self-proclaimed role as guarantor of world peace? In the event, it could and did – in the form of what we have come to know as peacekeeping. But this was an entirely different creature from the full-bloodied collective security based on central enforcement envisioned in the Charter.

The end of the Cold War: collective security at last?

If this full scale collective security was hamstrung by the political geometry of the Cold War and the polarized world that it created, then logically the passing of that era might have been expected to open up (or, more correctly, revive) some intriguing possibilities. If the robust and comprehensive system of military enforcement envisaged in 1945 had been frozen by the international politics of the time, surely the international politics of a new time would simply unfreeze it. Events in the Middle East in 1990 and 1991 seemed briefly to suggest that this might be so. The global response to Iraq's invasion of Kuwait in August 1990, which came amid the high rhetoric of a new world order from both George Bush in Washington and Mikhail Gorbachev in Moscow, raised hopes for a new multilateralism becoming lodged in the Security Council. Operation Desert Storm, as the American-led response to Iraq's aggression was known, won legitimization by a united Security Council. The action was not undertaken 'by' the UN under Chapter VII, but it still spoke of a new shared worldview among the permanent members of the Council. Superficially, the relationship of the United Nations to the conflict was very similar to that at the time of Korea, but the benevolent stance of the Soviet Union in

OPERATION DESERT STORM: SECURITY COUNCIL RESOLUTION 678 (NOVEMBER 1990)

The Security Council

Acting under Chapter VII of the Charter,

1. *Demands* that Iraq comply fully (with previous resolutions calling for its withdrawal from Kuwait) and decides, while maintaining all its decisions, to allow Iraq one final opportunity as a pause of goodwill to do so;
2. *Authorizes* member States co-operating with the Government of Kuwait, unless Iraq on or before January 15, 1991 fully implements the foregoing resolutions, to use all necessary means to uphold and implement Security Council Resolution 660 and all subsequent relevant resolutions and to restore international peace and security in the area;
3. *Requests* all States to provide appropriate support for the actions undertaken in pursuance of paragraph 2 of this resolution;
4. *Requests* the States concerned to keep the Council regularly informed of the progress of actions undertaken pursuant to paragraphs 2 and 3 of this resolution;
5. *Decides* to remain seized of the matter.

1990–1991 set the politics of the two conflicts far apart. Three of the P5, Britain and France along with the US, provided armed forces for the ensuing war – which secured the UN's stated objective: the removal of Iraqi forces from Kuwait.

The role of the UN as legitimizer rather than initiator of the military action against Iraq could be seen in less optimistic terms, however. For critics of the American-driven policy of the Security Council the Gulf War was more about the pursuit of Western interests than a herald of truly collective security. The difference between 1950 and 1990, as noted, was that the Soviet Union did not oppose the action. But this was a time of great political and diplomatic weakness for Moscow – in fact the very existence of the Soviet Union was in question. Was the Gulf War then less a new dawn for the authority and power of the UN than simply a one-off episode in an international system?

As international politics played out in the 1990s and into the new century the sceptical view seemed to be justified. The UN's role in the wars driving the break-up of Yugoslavia was restricted at least in part by an East–West division, not now based on competing political ideologies, but on historical ethnic affinities (with Russia rediscovering its pan-Slav sympathies for Serbia). In 1999, when collective action was taken over Kosovo, it is telling that it was done through the agency of NATO – the Western alliance – rather than the UN Security Council where Russia was once again willing and able to use its veto in its own national interests and those of its friends. As a result, the UN was brought in to the Kosovo situation only in the aftermath of the military action.

By the turn of the millennium it seemed clear that the difficulty for collective security on the original Charter model was not just one of global polarization. A much deeper resistance to UN multilateralism was rooted firmly in the international system. The irreducible fact was that in a stubbornly enduring world of sovereign states, UN members would continue to follow their own international political and security objectives in their own ways. States alone would continue to decide the extent to which those interests might be delegated to inter-governmental bodies such as the United Nations.

Subsequent international crises and the UN's response to them seemed to confirm this. In 2003 the United States and its allies (particularly perhaps Britain) would have much preferred UN legitimization of their invasion of Iraq. But when it became clear that this would not be achieved there was absolutely no question that they would pursue their military plan regardless. Later, in 2006, the Israeli invasion of Lebanon was not met with the firm response from the Security Council that the majority of UN members would have wished. The American administration did not share the majority view and the possibility of an American veto in the Security Council ensured inaction. A very similar situation prevailed at the beginning of 2009 following Israel's invasion of the densely populated and impoverished Gaza Strip. Meanwhile, in 2008 the UN had also been neutered by the anticipation of a veto from the opposite side of the old Cold War divide during Russia's short sharp war against Georgia over South Ossetia. In short, the end of the Cold War had done nothing to resolve the fundamental historical tension between sovereignty and collectivism in matters of national and inter-national security.

Disarmament and arms control

Underlying the UN's original model of collective security is the idea of progressive disarmament at the national level. As respon-sibility for the security of states passed from the unilateral to the multilateral plane these states would be required to give up their own national arsenals. While this remains utterly unattainable for as long as any viable collective security system remains merely a distant ambition, the United Nations has been active in various aspects of multilateral disarmament and the control of existing arms. It has notched up some real successes in the process.

Progressive international disarmament of course was not a new idea when the UN was formed. The Hague disarmament talks in 1899 and 1907 marked an important stage on the road

GENERAL ASSEMBLY RESOLUTION 1, 24 JANUARY 1946

Establishment of a Commission to deal with the problem raised by the discovery of Atomic Energy

Resolved by the General Assembly of the United Nations to establish a Commission, with the composition and competence set out hereunder, to deal with the problems raised by the discovery of atomic energy and other related matters:

...

The Commission shall propose with the utmost despatch and enquire into all phases of the problem, and make such recommendations from time to time with respect to them as it finds possible. In particular, the Commission shall make specific proposals

(a) for extending between all nations the exchange of basic scientific information for peaceful ends;

(b) for control of atomic energy to the extent necessary to ensure its use only for peaceful purposes;

(c) for the elimination from national armaments of atomic weapons and of all other major weapons adaptable to mass destruction;

(d) for effective safeguards by way of inspection and other means to protect complying States against the hazards of violation and evasions.

...

The work of the Commission should proceed by separate stages, the successful completion of each of which will develop the necessary confidence of the world before the next stage is undertaken.

towards global international organization, though plainly in view of the events of the following decade they were unsuccessful in saving the world from general conflict. Disarmament had also been a major international theme during the years of the League of Nations, though again discussions made no impact on the world's capacity to make war. The arrival of the United Nations however brought not just a predictable intensification of the drive to make disarmament meaningful; the advent of nuclear weapons (and the shock of their use in Japan at the end of the Second World War) gave a new urgency to the situation. This was reflected in the fact that the first ever resolution of the General Assembly in January 1946 established an International Atomic Energy Commission (IAEC) and called for nuclear disarmament.

The Charter gives special responsibility to the General Assembly for encouraging disarmament agreements among UN members (article 11) while the Military Staff Committee of the Security Council was supposed to be responsible for managing the processes involved (article 47). The onset of the Cold War, however, complicated the UN's role. Proposals coming from one side would almost invariably be rejected by the other as either political gestures or attempts to gain national advantage.

The American Baruch Plan, named for its main architect Bernard Baruch who was a special adviser to President Truman, was a classic example of this. It was presented at the first meeting of the new UN Atomic Energy Commission in 1946. It urged a system of free exchange of nuclear knowledge on the basis that it would be used only for peaceful purposes. Additionally, the UN would supervise future uranium production and distribution. Most remarkably, the Americans would undertake to pass control of their nuclear arsenal to the United Nations on the understanding that no other country would develop atomic weapons. The Baruch Plan was, in many respects, startlingly radical. But it was nevertheless rejected by a suspicious Soviet

Union. Moscow was concerned that the United Nations which would take control of nuclear weapons was (then) dominated by Western states. The whole project, the Soviet Union claimed, was designed to deprive it of parity in nuclear capacity while safeguarding American domination of atomic power.

The polarized atmosphere of the developing Cold War was of course fundamentally uncongenial to the idea of disarmament. But the very existence of such high levels of tension was a spur to the UN in its search for processes which would help meet the nuclear dangers involved in the East–West confrontation. In 1952 the General Assembly established the United Nations Disarmament Commission which provided a useful forum for discussion, though frequently it also provided a stage for public posturing by the superpowers. One of the bolder proposals explored by the Commission was the Rapacki Plan of 1957. This was sponsored by the Polish foreign minister, Adam Rapacki, and aimed to create a nuclear-free zone in central Europe. The intention was for this to extend gradually by a process of mutual roll-back of weapons by East and West. Just as the Baruch Plan had been rejected as a Western manoeuvre by Moscow, the Rapacki Plan was given short shrift by the West. The United States and its European allies saw it as part of a Soviet-inspired attempt to remove a crucial tool of NATO leverage on the geographic frontline of the Cold War. The nuclear-free space created would, it was argued, quickly be filled up by the numerically superior conventional forces of the Eastern bloc.

The Disarmament Commission did provide an important platform for longer term negotiations to limit nuclear confrontation. These led in 1963 to the UN's first major achievement in arms control. The Partial Test Ban Treaty outlawed nuclear testing in the atmosphere, underwater and in outer space. The treaty was important less for the actual obligations it placed on its signatories than what it seemed to say about the possibilities of further East–West agreement. In reality, by 1963 thermo-nuclear technology had already reached a point where the destruction of the planet would be easily achieved in a conflict; in a sense further testing was not critically important – and could still be carried out underground anyway. The real nuclear competition was now about means of delivering the devices rather than the power of the devices themselves. Nevertheless, coming, perhaps not by accident, after the shock of the Cuban missile crisis of 1962, the treaty was important to the extent that it gave some stability to the political relationship between the Cold War blocs.

During the 1960s the Disarmament Commission became eclipsed as the superpowers increasingly excluded third parties from their arms control discussions. As with peacekeeping, there was a permitted space for the UN in these discussions which contracted at this point. However, in 1968 the UN did have a central role in the landmark – and today still politically highly charged – Nuclear Non-Proliferation Treaty (NPT). This was ostensibly a small power initiative proposed in the General Assembly by Ireland. It would have died at birth like the Baruch and Rapacki Plans had it not been seen by the nuclear powers of the time – who happened to be the five permanent members of the Security Council – as in their own interests. The treaty requires signatories who already possess nuclear arms not to transfer either the weapons themselves or the technology to develop them to non-nuclear states. For their part, the non-nuclear countries undertake not to receive or seek such transfers or to establish their own nuclear weapons programmes.

Although the terms of the treaty also include a commitment to pursue general disarmament negotiations this is vague and peripheral. The treaty's evident intention was to freeze the global spread of nuclear weapons rather than to reduce existing stockpiles. Understandably, this has given rise to the complaint that it was designed primarily to consolidate the power of the

five existing nuclear states in 1968 and to prevent challenges
from beyond this privileged circle. Moreover, sovereign states
may choose not to adhere to the NPT as they can any other
treaty. India, Pakistan and Israel, known to have acquired
nuclear weapons since the treaty was first launched, have simply
declined to sign up to it. Yet for all its manifest shortcomings in
intent and effect, the NPT, now bearing 189 state signatories,
has had an enduring place in international relations for the past
four decades. Signatory states, most notably Iran, who may be
developing nuclear programmes, still feel constrained by the
NPT and it is at least possible that others have simply decided
that to publicly break their commitment would do unacceptable
damage to that intangible but always important international
currency, national prestige. North Korea, which first signed and
then withdrew from the treaty, was acting within its rights under
international law, but it was an expensive gesture for little real
profit. More positively, South Africa, which developed a nuclear
weapons capability in the 1970s during the apartheid years
apparently with Israeli help, belatedly signed the NPT in 1991
on the eve of majority rule and after destroying its weapons
stock. On the other side of the nuclear relationship, adherence
to the treaty has almost certainly constrained those powers
with capability from transferring nuclear technology to their
allies and clients; at all events, the NPT will have provided them
with a powerful excuse for not doing so when pressure has
been applied.

Although the Disarmament Commission was relaunched
following the General Assembly Special Session on
Disarmament in 1978, its subsequent contribution to arms
reduction has been limited. Based at the League's old headquarters in the Palais des Nations in Geneva, the Commission
currently meets only for a three week session each year and it has
pursued no initiatives of major significance for some time. Once
again, the issue is one of the space which big states allow to

multilateral organizations in areas seen to be of critical national importance. Even during the years of détente in the 1970s when the superpowers were willing to co-opt various UN functions to help manage their improved relationships, they tended to keep the more meaningful disarmament negotiations of the time – notably the Strategic Arms Limitation Talks (SALT) – between themselves and their allies. Similarly, the agreements of the late 1980s in the run-up to the end of the Cold War were made between Washington and Moscow with minimal involvement by international organizations. Where the UN's disarmament initiatives have been perceived to conflict with national interests they have tended simply to be ignored or accepted only by some states. United Nations attempts to outlaw completely the manufacturing and stockpiling of biological and chemical weapons and anti-personnel mines, for example, have been only partially successful for this reason.

While the achievements of the United Nations as an institution in the search for global disarmament have been limited, they have not been negligible. The UN's contribution to the process has been similar to its experience with the use of force in pursuit of peace. Both peacekeeping and disarmament initiatives have had to develop amid the constraints of an international system of sovereign states. Where the opportunity has arisen – whether for peacekeeping in the Middle East or for a Non-Proliferation initiative – the UN has usually been quick to seize it and has generally made a success of the ensuing process. Its failures have not, for the most part, been institutional; they have been contingent on the realities of life in what the international theorist Hedley Bull memorably described in the title of his celebrated study of international relations in 1977 as an 'anarchical society' of states.

4

Peace II: Peace-keeping and humanitarian intervention

Although United Nations peacekeeping is often seen as having emerged to fill the space left in the organization by the failure of coercive collective security, it has a longer pedigree. Undoubtedly though, the experience of Korea gave a much greater political impetus to the development of peacekeeping. In 1948 and again the following year, the UN had provided military observers to supervise ceasefires following regional wars. The first of these was in the Middle East after the fighting that erupted with the declaration of the state of Israel. Then, in 1949 war broke out between the new states of India and Pakistan over the disputed territory of Kashmir. At the time the despatch of military observers to these theatres just seemed to be pragmatic ad hoc responses to particular problems. But in retrospect they can be seen to have provided the basic outlines for the peace-keeping role that would become increasingly important during the Cold War. After the Cold War, peacekeeping, or humanitarian intervention as it came to be known in particular cases, became the UN's most high profile activity.

Classic UN peacekeeping supposedly demonstrates three ideal characteristics. First, the United Nations should only peacekeep with the full consent of the parties to the conflict it is intended to help resolve. Second, the military presence of the United Nations must be wholly neutral in the conflict and the politics surrounding it. Third, UN peacekeepers should use force only in self-defence and in the last resort.

The limitations of this model are obvious if the actual experience of recent UN peacekeeping is explored, however. The big operations of the 1990s and 2000s have rarely matched up to the ideal. Peacekeeping and humanitarian intervention, for example in Bosnia, Somalia, Rwanda and East Timor, has taken place when the consent of the local antagonists was at least doubtful. The UN also tends to have a particular political agenda, however implicit, involving the nurturing of democracy and the promotion of largely Western conceptions of human rights when it becomes involved in complex conflicts. Moreover, the use of force beyond a narrow definition of self-defence is often unavoidable if a UN operation is to be successful. In recent years, following the Rwanda genocide and the massacre of Bosnian Serbs in the supposed safe-area of Srebrenica, the UN has evolved a new doctrine of 'responsibility to protect' (or R2P in the spreading text-speak of the times). This places an obligation on UN forces to protect civilians in conflict situations, which greatly widens the rules of engagement from mere self-defence.

At the outset though, the charm of peacekeeping was precisely that it gave the UN an important military role in maintaining international peace without miring it in the political quicksand of Chapter VII–based collective security. In this way the peacekeeping role proved to be an important element in the organization's survival at a critical time in world politics. Where the enforcement model of Chapter VII required the identification of an aggressor, peacekeeping merely had to identify a conflict. Where Chapter VII cut across the idea of national sovereignty by requiring the participation of UN members, peacekeeping is a voluntary activity. And, while the original idea of UN force saw a military outcome and an imposed solution, peacekeeping is about stabilization and the creation of the necessary space for consensual peacemaking.

The logic of collective security requires that the lead be provided by the big powers. The ideal peacekeeper, in contrast, is a small or – best of all – a 'middle power'. While small powers are the least threatening to host countries, they may not have the necessary resources to carry out the military requirements of an operation. A middle-range state – such as Canada, Norway or India – will have the necessary material capacity but will still present no external threat in delicate conflict situations. During the Cold War the idea of the middle power peacekeeper had a political as well as a resource dimension. Neutral states, or at least ones perceived as distanced from bloc leaders, were favoured as peacekeepers, with formal neutrals such as Sweden, Ireland and Finland being particularly in demand. This careful selection of peacekeeping contributors, along with the requirement for the consent of the parties in a conflict, was designed to keep the larger global agendas of the biggest powers out of the process.

For all its importance to the organization, peacekeeping lacks one important attribute of the original model for collective security in the UN: it has no clear legal basis. The word

PEACEKEEPING DEFINED (UN DEPARTMENT OF PEACEKEEPING OPERATIONS)

Peacekeeping is a way to help countries torn by conflict create conditions for sustainable peace. UN peacekeepers – soldiers and military officers, civilian police officers and civilian personnel from many countries – monitor and observe peace processes that emerge in post-conflict situations and assist ex-combatants to implement the peace agreements they have signed. Such assistance comes in many forms, including confidence-building measures, power-sharing arrangements, electoral support, strengthening the rule of law, and economic and social development.

peacekeeping appears nowhere in the Charter. This lack of a precise legal identity caused real problems as peacekeeping grew in importance during the Cold War. Always sensitive to the danger of being isolated in the organization, the Soviet Union was very suspicious of what it saw as an ad hoc and unplanned military role being slipped in to the UN's functions. How was peacekeeping to be managed and controlled? The Military Staff Committee which would have taken command of actions under Chapter VII (had any ever been mounted), would have had a powerful Soviet presence. But this new legal orphan was bound by no firm rules. One effect of Moscow's misgivings was a major financial crisis for the UN when the Soviet Union (with some support from France) refused to accept that peacekeeping should be funded from the UN budget. The situation was only fully resolved after the end of the Cold War – by which time the United States too had fallen badly into arrears.

Against this ambiguous constitutional background there has been a certain amount of after-the-event thinking aimed at finding at least some kind of legal basis for peacekeeping. This usually focuses on Chapter VI of the Charter which, building towards the final resort of Chapter VII, deals with the 'Pacific Settlement of Disputes'. Two articles of Chapter VI seem to approach the idea of what developed as peacekeeping. Article 33 requires 'the parties to any dispute, the continuance of which is likely to endanger the maintenance of international peace and security' to 'seek a solution by negotiation, enquiry, mediation, conciliation, arbitration, judicial settlement, resort to regional agencies or arrangements, or other peaceful means of their own choice'. The Security Council itself though, under article 36, can also take the initiative, 'at any stage of a dispute of the nature referred to in Article 33 or of a situation of like nature'. In doing so it can 'recommend appropriate procedures or methods of adjustment'. The linking rods between these articles and the operational reality of peacekeeping are very tenuous, however.

Reflecting the frustration of this search for formal legitimization, peacekeeping has sometimes been described as a chapter six-and-a-half activity. This places it between the voluntary efforts to find pacific settlements to disputes urged in Chapter VI and the robust response of Chapter VII to breaches of the peace and acts of aggression. While this description encapsulates the essence of peacekeeping quite neatly, it is of course legally meaningless. Nevertheless, peacekeeping operations and humanitarian interventions lie at the centre of public awareness of the UN and are likely to remain so as demands for interventions continue.

Although the military observer missions which were established in the Middle East and Kashmir in the late 1940s were undoubtedly peacekeeping operations, the beginning of what is often regarded as real UN peacekeeping is more usually dated from 1956. In that year the United Nations Emergency Force (UNEF) was sent to Suez after the Anglo-French and Israeli invasion which followed the nationalization of the canal by Egypt. The conspiracy between the three countries to attack Egypt caused a storm of protest over what appeared to be an act of neocolonialist aggression. This indignation cut across normal Cold War loyalties. The United States was especially angered by its allies' recklessness, and encouraged the UN to find a way out of the crisis. The architects of this were Secretary-General Dag Hammarskjöld and the Canadian foreign minister, Lester Pearson. They proposed an intervention by an international force of contingents volunteered by UN members. This would be interposed between the two sides and would supervise a ceasefire and military disengagement.

The operation was in key respects just a larger-scale version of the military observer missions already in the field in the Middle East and South Asia. It was to be a substantial force rather than just a monitoring effort but the underlying principles of neutral supervision and moral presence were the same. UNEF would not take sides in the underlying conflict. This political neutrality underpinned one of the main elements of all successful peacekeeping since: the warring parties in the conflict could interpret and represent the operation in their own way. For Egypt, UNEF was there to stop the aggression of the invaders. Britain and France in contrast could claim to be handing the Suez problem over to the UN after providing the essential first rapid reaction to Egypt's illegal act of nationalization. In Suez there was never any likelihood that the UN force would find itself in a physical confrontation with any of the parties. They were all members of the UN, all had agreed to the deployment of the force and they were anxious to be seen as responsible citizens of the larger international community.

Two years later Hammarskjöld drew on the lessons of UNEF to offer a model of the new peacekeeping project. In this Summary Study the trio of key peacekeeping principles – neutrality, consent and minimum force in self-defence – was laid out in detail. The formal legal basis of peacekeeping was left no clearer however, and the coming decades were to see UN peacekeeping drawn into the larger Cold War conflict as an activity generally supported by the West but viewed with suspicion if not outright hostility by the Soviet bloc.

Peacekeeping in the Cold War

The fundamental task of peacekeeping in the Cold War period was to ease the often interlinked contemporary pressures of a polarized world and decolonization. Together these often appeared to threaten the fundamental fabric of the international state system. The purpose of UN intervention was primarily to inoculate local conflicts against larger global infections and this immunization was designed to work in two directions. Brushfires, as they were often described, should be contained to prevent their raging out of control and causing more death and destruction as proxy conflicts in the Cold War. Simultaneously though, these crises must not be allowed to draw the super-powers into local conflicts which would heighten hostility between them.

In the years after the Suez crisis of 1956 the UN carried out this task quite effectively. In Lebanon in 1958 and then again in Yemen in 1964 UN operations helped contain local conflicts which might otherwise have drawn in the superpowers. These operations, like the one in Suez, followed the classic peacekeep-ing model. They were either observation or interposition missions which stuck closely to the principles of consent, neutrality and (in the event unnecessary) self-defence. Importantly, they were also directly concerned with the security and integrity of international borders.

Simultaneously however, larger UN operations were taking place in other parts of the world which did not follow the set pattern nearly so closely. These throw into question the propos-ition that peacekeeping took a fundamentally new direction after the end of the Cold War. Between 1960 and 1964, for example, the huge UN operation in the former Belgian Congo (now the Democratic Republic of Congo where UN peace-keepers were again in action in the twenty-first century) was in place primarily to manage the collapse of the post-colonial state. It did so in an environment in which the limits of consent, neutrality and non-use of force were constantly being probed (and often crossed). As the Congo operation wound down, a new commitment was taken up in Cyprus. This was primarily concerned with inter-ethnic conflict inside the territory of the Cypriot state. While both the Congo and Cyprus crises had international implications, they were not inter-state operations. In the Congo moreover, the UN intervention was a multifunc-tional one with humanitarian aspects which went beyond trad-itional peacekeeping. This multifunctionality was even more evident in 1962–1963 in West New Guinea when the UN organized and controlled the transfer of the territory which had remained under Dutch colonial rule to Indonesia. Here, what was in effect a temporary UN state was established which had responsibility not just for security but for all government functions during the transition period. In other words, the classic ideal of Cold War peacekeeping was just that – an ideal difficult to locate in reality.

During the period of détente between the superpowers in the 1970s, the political setting in which United Nations interventions took place changed somewhat. By the end of the 1960s the United States and the Soviet Union had reached a point in their relationship which brought an understanding of their inescapable vulnerability to each others' nuclear capability (summed up by the famous acronym MAD – mutually assured destruction). This led to an interlude – in the event, a relatively short-lived one – in which the United Nations and its peacekeeping resources were co-opted by the superpowers in their mutual self-interest. The lead came here from the American secretary of state Henry Kissinger, but it was willingly followed by his Soviet counterpart Andrei Gromyko. And the UN secretary-general of the time, Kurt Waldheim, seemed happy to put the organization at their disposal. The superpowers themselves now took the lead in the process of quarantining regional conflicts from global rivalries. They did so by keeping their respective clients at more of a distance and looking to third party, often UN, management of potential conflicts.

This détente peacekeeping was most in evidence in the Middle East. After the 1973 Arab–Israeli war UN missions were deployed between Israel and Egypt (in Sinai) and Israel and Syria (on the Golan Heights). In both cases the driving force was the superpowers rather than the United Nations itself. This situation was in some ways questionable. In one respect, of course, it was better to have UN peacekeepers in place than not have them at all. But was it desirable for the UN to have its peacekeeping activities directed in this way by the superpowers for their own purposes? What did this say about the independence of the United Nations in world politics?

So far as this was a serious dilemma, however, it was a relatively short-lived one. In 1978 the UN intervened in Lebanon after the civil war and Israeli invasion. Again, the hand of American policy makers was in evidence. By this point, however, the détente between the superpowers was already beginning to unravel. Increasingly Washington and Moscow were reverting to unilateral support of clients rather than mutual control of them through third party intervention. The UN Interim Force in Lebanon (UNIFIL) suffered as a result of this dwindling of super-power support. On the larger stage, the end of détente meant that no UN operation would be established for the entire decade following the creation of the Lebanon force. Peacekeeping re-emerged, rather dramatically, only after the Cold War.

Peacekeeping since the Cold War

Whatever the fate of the UN's original vision for the enforce-ment of peace and security after the end of the Cold War, there was certainly a huge surge in its peacekeeping activities from the early 1990s onwards. This was the result both of new opportun-ities and new demands. On the positive side, the United Nations could now intervene on a much wider field as the restrictions of the Cold War were relaxed. Peacekeeping has always been contingent on the space (in both the geographical and political senses of the word) allowed to it. Where powerful states see critical national interests at stake, multilateral interven-tion whether by the UN or any other body will not be accept-able. The permitted space for peacekeeping expanded and contracted during the Cold War depending on the state of superpower relations. In the 1950s and 1960s these were often difficult. There was, consequently, no suggestion of UN peace-keepers being sent to Vietnam, or to Eastern Europe for that matter. These areas were too close to the core interests of the superpowers and therefore off-limits. During the years of détente, in contrast, the space widened a little. But then for most of the 1980s when the Cold War was particularly intense, it narrowed to a point where, as already said, peacekeeping was virtually dormant. The end of the Cold War therefore hugely expanded the field within which the United Nations could intervene. Central America and Southeast Asia, for example, which had previously been taboo regions, were now opened up to UN peacekeepers.

From *An Agenda for Peace* to the Brahimi Report

If these were the opportunities created by the end of the Cold War, there was a less positive side to the expansion of UN peace-keeping as well. During the Cold War the superpowers had, so to speak, kept their own houses in order by imposing stability on their respective spheres of influence. In Somalia, for example, American backing had helped keep the regime there in power despite strong undercurrents of domestic opposition. But with the end of the Cold War Somalia's critical strategic importance to the United States ended and American influence was withdrawn. The result was the rapid collapse of the state as rival factions now felt able to make their bids for power. The ensuing humanitarian crisis was left, initially at any rate, for UN peacekeepers to try to sort out. United Nations intervention therefore did not just become possible where it had not been possible before, it also became necessary in areas which had previously been relatively stable.

There were other pressures on UN peacekeeping resources which coincided with the end of the Cold War. Even in parts of the world where Cold War politics had not been particularly significant, such as West and Central Africa, many post-colonial states were in crisis. Once again, it was left to the UN to deal with the resulting conflicts as the superpowers and the former colonial powers resisted direct involvement. As a result, unprecedented United Nations resources had to be deployed in frequently intractable and apparently endless conflicts from Angola and Rwanda to Liberia and Sierra Leone.

In 1992, in an attempt to confront this situation as it developed, the then UN secretary-general, Boutros Boutros-Ghali, produced an important discussion document, *An Agenda for Peace: Preventive Diplomacy, Peacemaking and Peacekeeping*. This was the first significant contribution to the discussion of peacekeeping from within the organization since Hammarskjöld's Summary Study in 1958. Boutros-Ghali urged the fundamental reform of the management and funding of peacekeeping. This was essential, he argued, because of the new demands for UN intervention and the particular complexity of the conflicts that had now to be resolved. The old, essentially ad hoc approach, was no longer viable. The Agenda's proposals included formal contributors' agreements which would tie UN members to particular obligations along with a large reserve fund to meet the constant budgetary demands of peace operations. More controversially, although he still regarded the old ambitions of Chapter VII enforcement to be unachievable, Boutros-Ghali suggested the creation of a new form of UN force – 'peace enforcement units'. These would meet a growing problem for peacekeeping forces: the requirement to help implement peace agreements involving disarmament and demobilization of fighters which the signatories often did not honour. This has proved to be a major stumbling block for peace processes in Africa in particular. The new type of UN unit would be empowered to use force to compel compliance in these cases. Finally, Boutros-Ghali argued for a greater role for regional organizations which would be franchised by the United Nations to peacekeep in their own areas. Ideally, this would relieve the UN of some of the mounting burden of peace operations in the 1990s while encouraging regions to take greater responsibility for their own stability.

An Agenda for Peace was written at a time of relative optimism in the affairs of the United Nations. Unhappily, a series of high-profile peacekeeping failures followed, from Bosnia to Rwanda, and over the years few of the *Agenda*'s recommendations have been adopted. Member states have resisted blank cheque undertakings to participate in peacekeeping and have shown little enthusiasm for putting their soldiers in harm's way in peace enforcement activities. UN legitimized peacekeeping by non-UN bodies did become a limited feature of some regions, notably West Africa and the former Soviet Union. But it has been controversial, with accusations of political bias and the use of excessive force debasing the classic characteristics of the peacekeeping function. There have also been resource and capability problems associated with non-UN forces, well illustrated by the inadequate efforts of the African Union in Darfur. Nevertheless, coalitions of the willing organized by dominant regional states acting on behalf of the UN have proved effective. The Australian-led intervention in East Timor after the violence of 1999 was a good example of this.

The beginning of the new century saw another major report on the UN's peacekeeping role. This was commissioned by Boutros-Ghali's successor, Kofi Annan, and was produced by a panel led by former Algerian foreign minister Lakhdar Brahimi. The Brahimi Report of 2000 acknowledged the simple linguistic contradiction of most contemporary 'peacekeeping': operations tended to be undertaken in circumstances where there was in reality no peace to keep. In these situations the traditional trio of consent, neutrality and minimal self-defence are largely irrelevant. For Brahimi, the consent of the hostile parties was important, but its absence must not be allowed to rule out

Figure 5 Humanitarian Intervention in East Timor (UN Photo by Eskinder Debebe)

United Nations intervention. The UN has a responsibility to a wider public than specific warring factions. In other words, neither warlords nor dictators should be allowed a veto over the UN's attempts to secure peace.

On the question of the political objectivity of peacekeepers in the conflicts they deploy into, the Brahimi report made an interesting distinction between the concepts of 'impartiality' and 'neutrality'. Impartiality must mean respect for the principles of the UN Charter. But this is not the same as the neutral, equal treatment of all sides in all cases. The latter can amount to a policy of appeasement of wrong-doing. Debates about this dilemma within the United Nations and beyond had been underway since the advent of peacekeeping, but they had been given a new urgency after events in the 1990s. In Bosnia, for example, ethnic cleansing and the killing of civilians had taken place before the eyes of 'neutral' UN forces. One of the worst episodes of this had been at Srebrenica, a supposed UN-protected safe area, where some 8000 Muslim men and boys were massacred by Bosnian Serb forces while Protection Force peacekeepers stood by. As Brahimi put it, antagonists often 'consist not of moral equals, but of obvious aggressors and victims, and peacekeepers may not only be operationally justified in using force but morally compelled to do so'.[7] Although the expression was not used in the report, in making this point Brahimi was engaging with what would develop as the doctrine of 'responsibility to protect'.

It remains to be seen whether Brahimi's recommendations will be implemented by the UN and its members in a way that Boutros-Ghali's of the previous decade were not. On the positive side, as distance provides increasing perspective, it seems that the 1990s was a uniquely violent decade in many respects. So far in the twenty-first century United Nations peacekeepers have not been faced with the same number and intensity of conflicts. It may be that peacekeeping in the foreseeable future will be conducted in a calmer global environment which may be more suitable to innovative strategies and tactics. At the same time, some manifest failures of some peacekeeping in some places in the 1990s should not be allowed to detract from the basic success of a mechanism which, in sometimes very unpromising conditions, allows the United Nations to control, reduce and frequently resolve local conflicts which otherwise would cost many more lives and do much more damage to regional and global peace and security.

New concepts of sovereignty and intervention

As already observed, the classic view of peacekeeping presented by Dag Hammarskjöld was quickly proved unrealistic. But there was a reluctance to fully face up to this in the UN itself, whether at the upper levels of the Secretariat or among the membership. In part this was political expedience. To acknowledge a decisive departure from the principles of consent, neutrality and minimal force would be to place peacekeeping in a new and dangerous political plane. In particular, the increasing involvement of the UN in internal rather than international conflicts would have raised questions around the principle of state sovereignty. Even Boutros-Ghali's landmark *An Agenda for Peace* had approached this problem only obliquely and tentatively. More recently, however, a different perspective on the relationship between sovereignty and armed intervention by the UN has emerged. This envisages the United Nations using its peacekeeping capacity explicitly in the transmission and protection of universal norms and values within states and not just in the management of relations between states. The 'new peacekeeping' is supposedly novel in both operational terms and in its fundamental purpose.

Traditional peacekeeping was first and foremost an exercise in interposition. The UN would send soldiers who would insert themselves between states in conflict with each other. This might be done in a directly physical way where blue berets would occupy the land between two armies (UNEF in Suez is the classic example of this). Or it might be a less direct interposition in the form of military observers charged with confirming and monitoring ceasefires between hostile parties (as in Palestine and Kashmir). The new peacekeeping, it has been argued, is much more multifunctional and proactive. Peacekeepers, far from simply providing a largely passive moral presence, are now required to engage much more closely with the hostile parties, often overseeing programmes of disarmament and demobilization (and even the reintegration of former fighters into society). Peacekeepers may also be providers – or at least guarantors – of humanitarian aid in war zones.

More significant than any operational changes, though, is the transformation that may be taking place in the underlying political purpose of UN peacekeeping. Traditional peacekeeping was an instrument of international regulation, a means of oiling the machinery of the international state system. It sought to contain and defuse conflicts between states which might otherwise spin out of control and draw in other states. It provided a means of isolating brushfires before they spread. In contrast, the newer model of intervention is not primarily concerned with inter-state relations in the international system. It is designed to confront conflict in the world whatever its form and whoever the protagonists might be. In the contemporary world, conflict is much more likely to be between groups (ethnic, cultural, religious, regional etc.) than between states. This intra-state dimension is, according to those who advocate a new formulation of the rules and purposes of intervention, a defining characteristic of contemporary action by United Nations forces. The peacekeeper is not necessarily concerned directly with issues of global peace and security. The peacekeeper instead is engaged in a process of active conflict resolution (and, increasingly, post-conflict peacebuilding) rather than mere interposition.

The contending concepts of 'negative' and 'positive' peace come into the debate here. Traditional peacekeeping could be said to have as its primary objective the creation and maintenance of negative peace – simply the absence of physical violence. The new peacekeeping, in contrast, aspires more towards achieving positive peace, which is a much more comprehensive and multifaceted idea. The ideal state of positive peace goes beyond the end of actual violence to the long term harmony of social relations and the establishment of economic equity. The new peacekeeping, in other words, is not the surgical technique of the classic model, but one among a number of processes in a protracted therapy. The implications of this for the UN's attitude towards the sovereignty of its member states are obvious. In this view, states have no inherent right to dictate the social and political direction of UN intervention in their territories. Sovereignty in this perspective is qualified and conditional; it is not a legal absolute. Where a state fails to meet minimum standards of behaviour towards its own population then its sovereignty should be forfeit. Instead, the UN forces on the ground, legitimized by the international community, should have broad freedom of action to redress wrongs as well as to ensure the cessation of violence.

An underlying development which has helped drive this debate about the nature of contemporary peacekeeping is the deepening globalization of the world economy and, consequently, world politics. Economic and cultural globalization has fundamentally changed the nature of the international system in recent years. The traditional power of the state has been eroded by a global process which national politicians, however powerful, cannot control. At the same time, the revolution in communications underway since the late twentieth century has made geographical territoriality, a defining characteristic of sovereign statehood, much less significant in the real social and political world. While globalization is often regarded on the political left as a malign force which throws the poor and weak to the mercy of brutal market forces, it can also be seen to hold out a promise of a new global morality. It offers the prospect of a shift from a world politics based on a system of states to one built on a close-knit international community. In this alluring new world, independent statehood, and all the conflict created in its pursuit and protection over the past centuries, could be supplanted. This would not necessarily involve world government, but it would involve ever expanding mechanisms of ethically based global governance. What institution would be better placed to lead this trend, it is reasonably asked, than the United Nations?

Clearly, the implications of this for the UN go far beyond peacekeeping. They range widely across the spectrum of its activities, from international law and human rights to economic development and environmental cooperation. The idea of global governance is rooted in contemporary theories of cosmopolitanism (which means, literally, 'universal polity'). Cosmopolitanism claims the existence of a framework of essentially similar values shared by all humanity. At the centre of these lie the rights of the individual and not those of the state. Perhaps it is a reflection of this shift in attitudes, conscious or unconscious, that the term peacekeeping has increasingly been replaced in the UN and beyond by humanitarian intervention.

This vision of a new direction of travel for UN intervention is seductive. It suggests that the old view based on the sacred trio of neutrality, consent and non-use of force has been passed over by the march of history. But there is a dissenting position. Does a set of truly universal and unvarying human values actually exist? Or do different cultural, ethnic and religious groupings develop their own distinctive values? This more pluralist argument starts from the position that the international community is composed of a range of values and different attitudes to rights and that all are fundamentally legitimate. The danger, pluralists suggest, is that what are deemed by cosmopolitanists as universal values are in fact just the values of the dominant powers in the international system.

Within the United Nations conflicts can emerge between powerful members for ownership of the dominant values. For the Western members of the Security Council, for example, there should be no question that the UN should intervene militarily in Darfur to protect the population against attacks by the Sudanese state and its supporters. Universal values of human rights are at issue. But for China intervention in Darfur could amount to an attack on Sudanese sovereignty – and China regards non-interference in the business of sovereign states as at least as important a principle as human rights. Indeed, the imposition of moral positions from the outside can ultimately be seen as cultural imperialism rather than a defence of global norms. In some ways this is a debate which parallels one which has been particularly fraught recently in the domestic politics of Western countries faced with Islamist extremism within their own communities. Are there essential British (or French or Spanish) values and norms into which all members of these societies should be integrated? Or should the tenets of multiculturalism, the recognition and celebration of difference which has usually been seen as a progressive position, be allowed to continue? At the global level the argument has become central to discussions about the fundamental purposes of the United Nations in the contemporary world and its use of force in pursuit of them.

Viewed from a broad perspective, the UN's peacekeeping project has fallen far short of the ambitions the United Nations set itself in 1945. Collective security, enforced where necessary by military action under the leadership of the permanent members of the Security Council, remains as distant in the first part of the twenty-first century as it was in the middle of the twentieth. It was not merely Cold War bipolarity which prevented this, but a much more profound and long term preference among states for their own sovereignty over communal action. The United Nations itself can hardly be blamed for this enduring reality. The prospects for the new model of cosmopolitanist intervention by the UN remain uncertain. It is possible that we are entering a genuine new world order of a more profound character than that prematurely announced by President Bush at the end of the Cold War. But it is at least as likely that the visionaries of global governance have underestimated the power and persistence of state sovereignty in exactly the same way as their predecessors, the advocates of coercive collective security for the United Nations, did six decades earlier.

5
International law and human rights

The entire edifice of the United Nations is built on the foundation of international law. In signing the Charter, the precondition of membership, a country accepts a set of firm legal commitments. Member states are then invited additionally to sign up to a range of conventions and legal regimes. Established by the UN over the decades of its existence, these cover areas as diverse as the prohibition of genocide and maritime regulation. In this sense the UN generates international law. But it is also the major arbiter of international law.

This is another role among many that the UN inherited from the League of Nations. Although the idea of a world court of arbitration had been discussed even before the First World War (at the first Hague Disarmament conference in 1899), it was the League that brought it fully into being in the form of the Permanent Court of International Justice which, coincidentally, itself sat in the Hague. With the creation of the UN the name was changed to the International Court of Justice (ICJ), but its basic purpose and functions (and location) remained the same.

A world court?

The ICJ's own legal foundations are laid out in Chapter XIV (articles 92–96) of the Charter and in a special Statute appended to the Charter. The Court itself consists of fifteen judges whose

Figure 6 The International Court of Justice in The Hague (UN Photo by P. Sudhakaran)

appointments must be confirmed by both the Security Council and the General Assembly. No country can have more than one citizen as a judge at any one time. The judges serve for nine year terms, though they can be reappointed, and they elect the president of the Court from among their own number.

The ICJ has two basic functions. It is the in-house legal department for the United Nations system itself. In this role it can be asked by different parts of the organization to provide Advisory Opinions on the legality or otherwise of aspects of the UN's own work. In this sense it is the ultimate referee between contending interpretations of the Charter and other United Nations statutes. But the Court's more high profile and important role is to arbitrate between states in disputed areas of international law. Its judgements in these matters are in principle binding, and the failure of a state to adjust its policies in line with

ICJ findings could lead to the referral of the matter to the Security Council for the application of appropriate sanctions.

This arrangement does not look quite so robust in view of the fact that acceptance of the ICJ's jurisdiction is purely voluntary. Individual states choose whether or not they accept the compulsory jurisdiction of the Court. They may do this as a general principle or just in relation to specific treaties and agreements, and they may withdraw their acceptance of jurisdiction if they so choose at any time. Yet it is something of a testament to the status of international law that even in the absence of enforcement measures sixty-five states have made declarations accepting compulsory general jurisdiction (though admittedly most of them insist on some specific exclusion covering areas of special national interest). The reasons for this general acceptance of the Court's writ are both symbolic and practical. National prestige within the international system is widely seen by states to be enhanced by public acceptance of the rule of law. But more tangibly, states accept the ICJ's jurisdiction on the basis of the legal principle of reciprocity. The existence of an international court only makes practical sense if it operates in a community of states which are willing to comply with its judgements.

THE POWER OF THE ICJ (UN CHARTER ARTICLE 94)

1. Each Member of the United Nations undertakes to comply with the decision of the International Court of Justice in any case to which it is a party.
2. If any party to a case fails to perform the obligations incumbent upon it under a judgment rendered by the Court, the other party may have recourse to the Security Council, which may, if it deems necessary, make recommendations or decide upon measures to be taken to give effect to the judgment.

If there is no general culture of compliance, then the ICJ itself would be an irrelevance and its contribution to the orderly management of international relations non-existent.

Nevertheless, the fact that pronouncements of the Court do not have to be complied with by states unless they themselves submit to its jurisdiction is frequently brought in evidence of the emptiness of international law. And, it is certainly true that some high profile cases can confirm an impression that the big powers simply ignore the Court when it suits them. Currently, in fact, only Britain among the permanent members of the Security Council accepts compulsory jurisdiction. The casebook of the Court is not lacking in disputes where the big powers have simply disregarded its findings. A landmark opinion given by the Court in 1962 confirmed that peacekeeping, despite its lack of clear legal definition, was a regular activity of the United Nations and therefore subject to compulsory financial assessments. This did not suit Soviet policy towards peacekeeping – and it came at a critical time in the midst of the politically fraught Congo operation – so it was simply rejected by the Soviet Union. The result was long term problems for the management and financing of peacekeeping operations. Later, during the 'second' Cold War in 1984, the left-wing Sandinista government of Nicaragua took the United States to the ICJ over American mining of its harbours. The Court's judgement in favour of Nicaragua, far from bringing American compliance, led the Reagan administration to withdraw the United States from compulsory jurisdiction. Later, when the matter was transferred to the Security Council under article 94 of the Charter, the United States used its veto to block any further action.

Yet for all this superpower disdain, the great majority of the Court's judgements – on matters from frontier disputes in Latin America and North Africa to the disputed interpretation of treaties – are complied with. Despite the obvious shortcomings of its enforcement powers, the ICJ has made a solid contribution to the stability of international relations.

The UN and the law of the sea

One of the UN's main contributions to international law lies in its housekeeping role in the coordination and codification of existing laws which have evolved from different sources. By bringing specific areas – or 'regimes' – of laws together, ambiguities are ironed out and consistency of application can be guaranteed. There are about 500 UN conventions. These are in effect international treaties with multiple signatories who all accept them as legally binding. (Conventions of this type are the dominant form of contemporary humanitarian law.) Among the UN's most substantial exercises in the organization and reform of international law in a crucially important area is the Convention on the Law of the Sea. In many respects maritime law is an ideal area for regulation by a world body. The oceans, after all, cover about three-quarters of the world's surface area. The law of the sea also affects to some extent every country in the world, some critically. Many national economies are entirely dependent on the sea and the exploitation of its resources. The national security of many countries is closely tied to control of sea areas. All countries – even the landlocked – depend to some extent on maritime trade routes. Both literally and politically the sea connects states and therefore has always had a central role in international relations.

When the UN came into being, the law of the sea consisted of rules and norms which had developed haphazardly over the centuries. Many of these had acquired the status of law through customary practice. This is roughly the international law equivalent of common law in the domestic jurisdiction. Common law is not to be found in specific parliamentary legislation but is nevertheless law because it has historically been accepted as such. At the beginning of the twentieth century most countries accepted the principle of a three mile territorial limit from the shore over which state sovereignty could be exercised.

Everything beyond this consisted of the high seas, over which all nations had equal rights of passage and resource exploitation. The only customary rules applying to the high seas related to reciprocal responsibilities between mariners for their mutual safety and some special obligations such as the suppression of piracy and the slave trade. Yet how had the three mile limit been fixed, and how relevant was it to the increasingly technological world of the twentieth century? In fact it had originally been set in the seventeenth century on the basis of the range of shore artillery batteries; beyond three miles, it was agreed, the state could not effectively exercise its monopoly of power – a key criterion of sovereignty.

Increasingly in the twentieth century, states sought to extend their control of resources beyond the old limits. A number of countries began to view their portion of the continental shelf – the underwater geological platform on which a country's landmass sits – as a fairer marker of national sovereignty than an arbitrary and antiquated limit. Many states now began to set unilaterally their territorial sea limit at twelve miles (and some much further). Meanwhile, with the old certainties of the three mile limit in doubt, conflicts grew in areas where new self-declared maritime frontiers were particularly close.

The League of Nations made an attempt at codification of the law of the sea in the early 1930s but was ultimately overwhelmed by the complexities involved. The new United Nations set out to succeed in this just as in other areas where the League had failed. In 1958 a Law of the Sea Conference convened by the General Assembly produced four separate conventions dealing with the high seas, the continental shelf, territorial seas and fishing and marine exploitation. The conventions were an advance on the increasingly anarchic customary practice but key issues were still left unresolved. Consequently, in 1973 another conference began work under the auspices of the General Assembly. This worked slowly but steadily over most of the following decade to produce a new comprehensive United Nations Convention on the Law of the Sea in 1982.

The Convention was slow to be consolidated into law. But it represented a monumental contribution to international regulation. It is a landmark in the development by the United Nations of mechanisms of global governance. The twelve nautical mile territorial limit already set unilaterally by many states was formally adopted into law, though with the caveat that vessels of all nations had a right to 'innocent passage' through national waters. Beyond this territorial limit a further distance of twelve nautical miles would henceforward be considered as a 'contiguous zone' over which the state would have certain legal rights (to deal with smuggling of prohibited goods and the movement of illegal immigrants, for example). One of the most important parts of the Convention was the introduction of an Exclusive Economic Zone (EEZ). As well as control of the territorial limit and more limited powers in the contiguous zone, countries had the right to sole exploitation of maritime economic resources within a 200 nautical mile area measured from their shoreline. This of course has proved difficult in implementation because the many overlaps make this zone anything but exclusive in several parts of the world.

At the outset of negotiations on the Convention, the EEZ arrangement was seen as significant mainly for fishery rights. Even such normally friendly countries as Britain and Iceland had found themselves in violent conflict over fishing grounds (most dramatically in the famous Cod Wars which erupted intermittently between the 1950s and the 1970s) and mutually accepted regulation was clearly in everyone's interest. During the long course of discussions, however, the development of off-shore oil and gas extraction gave a new urgency to the search for a legal framework which would parcel out newly valuable marine resources in an orderly way. Meanwhile, the vexed issue of the continental shelf was dealt with by extending the exclusive right to economic exploitation beyond 200 miles where a country's off-shore shelf extended further than this distance to a maximum of 350 nautical miles from the shore.

The apparently leisurely pace at which the General Assembly conference arrived at the Convention (a period of nine years) reflects the special difficulties which are encountered in the formulation of new international law. The non-binding nature of international law and the absence of any conventional means of enforcement rules out even a majoritarian approach based on national votes – the dissenting minority of states are likely simply to withdraw from the process. Advances can only be made on the basis of consensus. This difficulty increases in proportion to the number of states involved, and in the case of the law of the sea negotiations this amounted to virtually the entire international system. The challenge for those presiding over the process, UN officials and national representatives, was to fix the correct balance between necessary compromise and excessive dilution. As it was, the United States refused to ratify the final Convention on the grounds that it did not adequately protect its economic and security interests. It has recently indicated, though, that it will probably soon do so. This in itself is perhaps a measure of the centripetal force for compliance with the mainstream which tends to be exerted by international legal arrangements that are widely but not universally accepted.

It would be wrong to be too upbeat about the advances brought by the UN to the law of the sea, however. The Convention on the Law of the Sea has been a huge improvement on the tangle of customary practices which preceded it but it is inevitably an imperfect instrument for the management of rival claims. For one thing, the simple but unchallengeable realities of geography come into play. Not many countries in the world have a coastline 400 miles from that of their neighbours. Few perch on their own exclusive continental shelves. The strategic importance of oil and gas reserves in a world rapidly running out of these conventional energy resources but yet to develop alternatives ensures that conflicts over marine reserves will continue and probably intensify. For example, British claims to the outcrop of Rockall which lies in the north Atlantic more than 460 kilometres from the Scottish mainland bring it into conflict with Ireland, Iceland and the Faeroes, who have their own claims. Britain also claims a 200 mile EEZ in the South Atlantic based on its sovereignty over the Falkland Islands. Unsurprisingly this is regarded by Argentina as a provocation. Conflicts and rivalries of this sort are to be found around the world and may simply be beyond remedy by international law.

Human rights

The issue of human rights had not featured prominently in the work of the League of Nations. In truth, the concept of universal individual rights was still a novel one outside a few Western democracies in the first half of the twentieth century. However, some aspects of the League's activities could be seen as precursors of the UN's focus on the area. The principle of national self-determination which pervaded the League's work pointed in the general direction of human rights, though the emphasis here was more on the collective political rights of nationalities rather than those of individual citizens. After the Second World War, a conflict which had been marked by wholesale abuse of civilian populations in Europe and in Asia up to and beyond the point of genocide, the global perspective shifted and this was inevitably reflected in the preoccupations of the world organization. In December 1948 the General Assembly proclaimed the Universal Declaration of Human Rights (UDHR) and invited member states 'to cause it to be disseminated, displayed, read and expounded principally in schools and other educational institutions, without distinction based on the political status of countries or territories'.

PREAMBLE TO THE UNIVERSAL DECLARATION OF HUMAN RIGHTS, 10 DECEMBER 1948

THE GENERAL ASSEMBLY proclaims THIS UNIVERSAL DECLARA-
TION OF HUMAN RIGHTS as a common standard of achievement
for all peoples and all nations, to the end that every individual and
every organ of society, keeping this Declaration constantly in mind,
shall strive by teaching and education to promote respect for these
rights and freedoms and by progressive measures, national and
international, to secure their universal and effective recognition
and observance, both among the peoples of Member States
themselves and among the peoples of territories under their
jurisdiction.

The UDHR was the fruit of the UN Commission on
Human Rights which had been set up in 1946 under the chairmanship of Eleanor Roosevelt, widow of the driving force in
the creation of the United Nations, President Franklin D.
Roosevelt. Always a formidable advocate of liberal causes, her
appointment to the position was motivated by much more than
just sentiment. The Declaration covers the range of rights now
familiar in most national constitutions. Beginning with the basic
right to life, liberty and security of the person, the UDHR goes
on to set out basic rights to freedom from slavery and torture and
to assert a range of family rights. It also sets basic political, legal
and employment standards which would be more correctly
described as civil rights.

The Declaration was adopted by the General Assembly with
no dissenting votes but its ratification by national governments –
and more importantly its universal implementation – has not
been so easily achieved. This has not just been due to repressive
and cynical governments, however. There is a basic conceptual
problem with the idea of universal rights, one closely allied
to the debate around cosmopolitanism and humanitarian

intervention touched on in the previous chapter. A frequent criticism of the human rights discourse in the United Nations is that it is driven by an essentially Western sensibility which is rooted in eighteenth-century European and North American liberalism. Communist states, for example, traditionally placed more focus on collective, communal rights rather than individual rights. For them the proper emphasis tended to be on 'freedoms from' – hunger, disease and so on. This corresponds to what political theorists, following the British philosopher Isaiah Berlin, would describe as positive freedom. It is the 'freedom to' express and conduct oneself as an individual – negative freedom – that has traditionally dominated human rights debates at the UN. This self-referential individualism is often denounced by Marxist politicians as an enemy of true freedom. That standpoint was often taken up by new states in the global South as they came to independence and faced the communal problems of underdevelopment. The absolute demands of economic development as a means of securing freedom from want will often be at odds with the personal rights of the individual.

Against this, of course, the advocates of individual rights will often point out that this justification for rejecting individuals' claims for rights is simply an alibi for their denial of rights to political opponents who would otherwise threaten their power and privileges. But there is a cultural and religious dimension to be considered as well which is perhaps less easily dismissed as self-serving. Theocratic states such as Saudi Arabia and Iran where civil politics are entwined with religious requirements and prohibitions (which often have strong popular support) may also reject claims of the universalism of personal liberties. Some such freedoms may not be recognized (or they may even be actively rejected) by particular religious credos. In short, what in one perspective are universal and non-negotiable rights are in another simply cultural imperialism.

KOFI ANNAN ON HUMAN RIGHTS
(*IN LARGER FREEDOM*, 2005)

Human rights are as fundamental to the poor as to the rich, and their protection is as important to the security and prosperity of the developed world as it is to that of the developing world. It would be a mistake to treat human rights as though there were a trade-off to be made between human rights and such goals as security or development. We only weaken our hand in fighting the horrors of extreme poverty or terrorism if, in our efforts to do so, we deny the very human rights that these scourges take away from citizens. Strategies based on the protection of human rights are vital for both our moral standing and the practical effectiveness of our actions.

Whatever the practical and philosophical issues involved, it is certainly true that the place of human rights in the work of the United Nations has grown since the end of the Cold War. Marxism and the national political systems which had challenged the idea of individual rights had lost to Western-style individualism, and the rhetoric of human freedom became louder at the UN. In 1993 it was possible for the first time to create the post of United Nations Commissioner for Human Rights. In the same year the first large-scale UN human rights conference took place in Vienna. Then, in 2006, the basic structure of human rights regulation in the UN was reformed when the venerable Human Rights Commission, originally answerable to the Economic and Social Council (ECOSOC), was replaced by the Human Rights Council which reported directly to the General Assembly.

This is potentially a very important reform, the effect of which has yet to become clear. It was an initiative of the then secretary-general, Kofi Annan, who was remarkably frank about the shortcomings of the Human Rights Commission. In his view, expressed in a landmark 2005 report on the future of the UN system, *In Larger Freedom*, the Commission had been 'undermined by its declining credibility and professionalism'.[8] He pinpointed the problem of states which had 'sought membership of the Commission not to strengthen human rights but to protect themselves against criticism or to criticize others'. This had now cast 'a shadow on the reputation of the United Nations system as a whole'. He was no doubt conscious here of, among other questionable developments, the election of Libya to the presidency of the Commission in 2003. Consequently, he proposed the abolition of the Commission and its replacement by the smaller, but more effective and authoritative Council which would take its place alongside the Security Council and the Economic and Social Council as a key agency in pursuing the objectives of the UN in the twenty-first century.

So far the new body, which began work in June 2006 after the abolition of the Commission, appears to have only partially met Annan's concerns. Its origins were not trouble-free. The Human Rights Council is directly accountable to the General Assembly rather than being a more or less free-standing body as the Commission had been. But this is not regarded by some states which are traditionally wary of the politics of the Assembly as a particularly effective reform. The United States and Israel, for example, voted against the new arrangement, not because they favoured a continuation of the old one, but because they did not see the depoliticization of human rights in the UN as going far enough. To hand responsibility to the General Assembly (which is traditionally hostile to American and Israeli policy in the Middle East) would, in their view, provide little in the way of greater impartiality. The Human Rights Council is only marginally smaller than the Human Rights Commission (with forty-seven rather than fifty-three seats) and like the Commission is elected on the basis of regional quotas. The predominance of countries of the global South in the Council means, from the perspective of the United States, that its criticisms (and notably those of Israel) remain one-sided and biased. This, Washington insists, distorts the reality of human rights observance, or lack of it, in the international system as a whole.

There is certainly the potential for the clash of different national perspectives on rights to generate political conflict rather than ease it. This was in evidence at a special UN conference against racism held under the auspices of the Human Rights Council in Geneva in April 2009. Both the United States and Israel had boycotted the event in advance, anticipating anti-Israeli pronouncements from many of the delegations. When, on cue, the Iranian president, Mahmoud Ahmadinijad, himself head of a state with a less than impressive record on individual rights, denounced Israel's behaviour in particularly savage terms, West European delegations walked out of the conference hall. The ultimate impact of the event was to set back international relations over the Middle East without noticeably advancing any human rights agenda.

The Western nations from whose cultural and political history the idea of universal rights supposedly emerged have not themselves always been absolutely faithful to the terms of the Universal Declaration. Political contingencies and pragmatism shape their compliance. Few countries can claim to have met in full the prohibitions in the Declaration against torture and cruel, inhumane and degrading treatment. Freedom from arbitrary arrest and detention, freedom of expression and of peaceful protest and respect for private correspondence are not accepted as absolutes in even those countries that place their commitment to liberty at the centre of their national values. And, depressingly, more than six decades after the adoption of the UDHR, some Western states seem to have regressed rather than advanced in their compliance. Pleas to the imperatives of national security and the demands of the 'war on terror' have been used to excuse a range of behaviour on the part of states whose inventive use of euphemism has done little to disguise the fact that they are acting in breach not only of their own national laws but the rules of international behaviour that they have publicly subscribed to.

In the late 1940s the widely different perspectives on rights among the membership of the UN hampered plans to set the Declaration as a starting point in a continuous process in which universal liberties would be identified and expanded. Over the

LANDMARK UN CONVENTIONS ON HUMAN RIGHTS

1948	Convention on the Prevention and Punishment of the Crime of Genocide
1966	International Convention on the Elimination of All Forms of Racial Discrimination
1966	International Covenant on Economic, Social and Cultural Rights
1966	International Covenant on Civil and Political Rights
1966	Optional Protocol to the International Covenant on Civil and Political Rights
1979	Convention on the Elimination of All Forms of Discrimination against Women
1984	Convention against Torture and Other Cruel, Inhumane or Degrading Treatment or Punishment
1989	Convention on the Rights of the Child
1989	Second Optional Protocol to the International Covenant on Civil and Political Rights, aiming at the abolition of the death penalty
1990	International Convention on the Protection of the Rights of All Migrant Workers and Members of their Families
2006	Convention on the Rights of Persons with Disabilities
2006	International Convention for the Protection of All Persons from Enforced Disappearance

years following the adoption of the UDHR, efforts were made to construct two more advanced and detailed covenants on, first, civil and political rights and, second, on economic, social and cultural rights. These were eventually adopted by the General Assembly in 1966, but only after a long and hard process of compromise; and, like the original Declaration, they are very far from commanding effective compliance.

The UN has had more success in the regulation – if not the enforcement – of specific areas of rights. The Genocide Convention of 1948, for example, commits signatories to take action to prevent or stop the crime of genocide wherever it may take place. It is a commitment taken at least semi-seriously by the major powers in the Security Council on which the chief responsibility for action would fall. In 1994, during the system-atic massacre of Rwandan Tutsis by their Hutu countrymen, the permanent members of the Council were forced into a tricky linguistic delicacy in order to avoid any use of the 'G' word. To formally utter it would, in principle, have committed them to robust action they were unwilling to take. Similarly, when in 2008 US State Department officials began to speak of genocide in Darfur, they did so in a wholly calculated way as a coded threat to the Sudanese government.

It would be wrong, though, to judge the impact of the UN's conventions simply on the basis of how many states agree to be bound by them and the extent to which they comply with the rules when they have done so. They have a less tangible, less measurable function as well which, in the long term, may prove to have been their greater contribution to the spread of human rights. The very existence of conventions creates its own momentum. By adopting a convention the General Assembly is sending a message worldwide about the existence of global norms. Such norms can only be effectively transferred and assim-ilated if they are first asserted. In this way the 1979 Convention on Sex Equality and the Convention on the Rights of the Child of 1989, for example, serve a purpose by simply existing. This does not, of course, solve the problem that such sets of rights can be seen as cultural impositions, but the universal nature of the General Assembly clearly lessens the impact of the accusation. And, while there may be a wide space between the adoption of a statement of rights and compliance with it by individual states, public awareness of standards that have been laid down internationally will always provide a pressure point for those who would hold governments to their commitments.

International criminal law

The Nuremberg trials of the major Nazi war criminals in 1945 and 1946 represented a dramatic departure for international law. For the first time something which could approximately be described as the international community had established a judicial process which held to account officials of a sovereign state for breaches of international law. The accusation that this process amounted to no more than one-sided victors' justice could be fairly easily countered. The existing architecture of international law – the Permanent Court of International Justice at that time being transformed into the UN's International Court of Justice – was simply inadequate to the task of applying post-war justice. Arbitration between consenting sovereign states was simply irrelevant to the extent and monstrosity of the crimes in question. As the final judgement at Nuremberg stated, 'crimes against international law are committed by men, not abstract entities, and only by punishing individuals who commit such crimes can the provisions of international law be enforced.'[9]

Yet for several decades afterwards Nuremberg and the other trials that followed the Second World War looked as though they would remain unrepeated legal events. In 1948 the General

Assembly established the International Law Commission (ILC) to pursue the extension of international law and its application under the UN system. An evident lack of energy and commitment to the project on the part of UN member states slowed this process virtually to a stop. The Commission consists of thirty-four members, all distinguished international jurists drawn from UN member states and elected for a five-year term. Established in the same year as the Genocide Convention, the ILC was charged with exploring 'the desirability and possibility of establishing an international judicial organ for the trial of persons charged with genocide'.[10] Despite producing a draft statute for such a court in 1951, the ILC could not itself engineer any advance towards its establishment. Just as the Cold War dogged the UN's ambitions for collective security, the polarized system also ruled out any international criminal tribunal. Specifically, the plans foundered on the failure of UN members to agree a definition of aggression in international relations – the same problem which confounded the application of enforcement under Chapter VII of the Charter. Permitting the ICJ the space to act as referee between consenting states was one thing, putting individuals in the dock for actions on behalf of their governments, Western or Communist, would have been quite another.

All this changed with the end of the Cold War. The 1990s saw special tribunals established by the United Nations to try those accused of criminal actions in the worst of the conflicts which stood out even in that especially bloody decade. The largest of these were for the former Yugoslavia and Rwanda, established by Security Council resolutions in 1993 and 1994 respectively. Initially, there was much cynicism about the project. To many, the establishment of the tribunals by the members of the Security Council had an air of guilty conscience about it. The permanent members had been criticized for inactivity and a lack of commitment to effective intervention throughout the Balkan wars and during the genocide in Rwanda. The tribunals could be seen as designed to recover the reputations and prestige of the big powers through an inexpensive and possibly rather empty gesture. The reality, at least eventually, did not quite justify this scepticism, though at the outset the performance of the tribunals was not impressive.

The Rwanda tribunal, which was convened in the northern Tanzanian town of Arusha, frequently seemed disorganized and unnecessarily slow in its deliberations. In this it compared unfavourably with Rwanda's own, rather more robust, national judicial process which also tried alleged *génocidaires* who had fallen into its hands. The tribunal for the former Yugoslavia, which sits in The Hague, was criticized during the early years of its work for its apparent concentration on defendants who were relatively low in the order of culpability (though on the horrific scale of the conflict, few could be considered minor criminals). There was a suspicion that the Western powers, whose NATO forces operated throughout Bosnia after the end of the war there in 1995, were not properly committed to hunt down and deliver the more important figures to The Hague. This seeming reluctance derived, some suspected, from a desire not to destabilize a delicate political settlement in the former Yugoslavia which was based on a very fragile peace. On a larger canvas, there may also have been a concern not to provoke Russia, which was becoming increasingly suspicious about Western intentions in the Balkans after the break-up of Yugoslavia and whose own resurgent nationalism embraced a long-standing pan-Slavism and an underlying sympathy for Serbia.

This changed dramatically when in 2002 a new reformist government in Serbia delivered none other than its former president, Slobodan Milosevic, to The Hague. Milosevic was in the view of many the principal malign force which had driven the Balkan wars of the 1990s. The NATO action against Serbia over Kosovo in 1999 which effectively ended these wars had proved the beginning of the end for Milosevic. His brand of extreme Serb nationalism had been a vote winner only as long as it delivered positive results for Serbia; ultimately though it had brought the loss of Kosovo and the destruction of much of Serbia's own infrastructure. This sealed his fate. Milosevic was obviously at the absolute top of the hierarchy of alleged war criminals, and public perceptions of The Hague tribunal were dramatically improved when he went on trial. The trial of Milosevic proceeded at a snail's pace over the next four years before ending dramatically with his sudden death from heart failure in early 2006. However, in the new climate in Serbia other major actors in the war followed Milosevic to The Hague, including another former president and Milosevic lieutenant, Milan Milutinovic. Then, in the summer of 2008, Serbian security police arrested Radovan Karadzic, the leader of the Bosnian Serb statelet which had been associated with the worst of the atrocities during the break-up of Yugoslavia in the early 1990s. Karadzic too was rapidly and unceremoniously handed over to The Hague tribunal.

The shifting fortunes of The Hague tribunal are instructive; they illustrate the absolute dependency of the UN's ambitions for international law on changing patterns of both national and international politics. Events, often unpredictable, in the domestic politics of states with an interest in particular trials, and broader changes in the diplomatic climate can determine success or failure for judicial processes. Serbia's change of heart towards cooperation with The Hague tribunal from the early 2000s was not due to any Damascene conversion to the ideals of global governance and the rule of international law through the United Nations. It was the result of Serbia's desperate economic plight after a decade of war and the determination of its new political leadership to end the country's isolation from the European and international mainstream. Specifically, Serbia was seeking economic support from the United States and eventual membership of the European Union. This provided the Western powers with unprecedented and irresistible leverage which quickly opened up the road to The Hague for previously protected indictees. When international criminal law and political imperatives collide, politics will invariably prevail; when they coincide, new possibilities appear. It falls to the United Nations to make the best of these possibilities (and usually, unjustly, to take the blame when politics trumps law).

In the later 1990s, in the wake of the ad hoc tribunals for the former Yugoslavia and Rwanda, political conditions appeared to favour the long dormant project of a permanent International Criminal Court (ICC). In many ways this seemed a natural continuation of the ad hoc tribunals. They had demonstrated that in the post-Cold War world individuals could be held to account for acts of international criminality, however imperfect the process might be. One-off courts for specific conflicts have inherent shortcomings, however. Like the post-war Nuremberg trials, they are open to the accusation of selectivity of justice: why are certain crimes in certain conflicts in certain places subject to the application of law and not others? Why Bosnia and Rwanda, but not the Democratic Republic of Congo or Iraq? In other words, a permanent tribunal would go some way to lessening the political domination of international justice. A separate Security Council resolution would not be required to begin proceedings for each separate conflict. The existence of a permanent institution would also enhance the deterrent effect of the judicial process by increasing the chances of individual criminals being pursued in what might be relatively low profile conflicts. This is important, as one of the major impediments to the rule of law in world conflicts is the pervading culture of impunity which has developed since the mid-twentieth century. As José Ayala Lasso, a UN High Commissioner for Human Rights, put it before the establishment of the ICC, a 'person stands a better chance of being tried and judged for killing one human being than for killing 100,000'.[11] The ad hoc tribunals are also time-limited in respect of the conflict with which they are dealing. The Security Council mandates empowering the Rwanda and former Yugoslavia tribunals set end dates for their jurisdiction, even though in both regions crimes continued even after the establishment of the tribunals. A permanent criminal court would be unrestricted in this way. Finally, a permanent ICC would offer economies of scale and efficiency in contrast to individual tribunals which had to constantly reinvent the wheel, administratively and legally speaking, as they were established.

Taken as a whole these various benefits of a new, permanent institution would provide what has been described as the missing link between ad hoc criminal tribunals able to try individuals in certain situations and the International Court of Justice which is permanent but which can only deal with states. Despite these compelling arguments, the creation of the ICC was far from trouble-free. A number of countries had misgivings about the proposed processes and jurisdiction of the court. The most important among these was the United States which, as the world's only remaining superpower, looked askance at the prospect of American soldiers or officials being subjected to international criminal proceedings outside the national jurisdiction. This American opposition though first expressed by the Clinton administration became much more pronounced under the presidency of George W. Bush which was ideologically hostile to this type of globalism. The prospects of American adherence to the Statute therefore dwindled further. From 2001, of course, the Bush administration was also engaged in a series of conflicts in Iraq, Afghanistan and more widely which at least in theory made American forces and their commanders particularly vulnerable to indictment by any international court.

While there was little doubt that a majority of UN members favoured the creation of the court, it could not be a meaningful institution without a critical mass of support. In the real political world, such mass is not provided simply by arithmetical majorities. Nevertheless, after a lengthy process of formal and informal discussion, the General Assembly held a special conference in Rome in the summer of 1998 at which the statute of the new International Criminal Court was adopted by 120 votes to seven with twenty-seven abstentions. Those voting against the statute formed an odd and unlikely alliance. They included two permanent members of the Security Council – the United States and China – along with Israel and Iraq (then still under Saddam Hussein). The Rome Statute came into effect in 2002, with the court coming into existence the following year with the appointment of eighteen judges.

As with the International Court of Justice, the authority of the ICC normally extends only to those countries voluntarily accepting its jurisdiction (some 106 states by 2008) and then only when national legal processes have not been pursued or have proved ineffective. In this sense, the ICC is a court of last resort. A number of important states which did not actively oppose the Rome Statute have nevertheless failed to ratify it. One of these is Russia, which means that three out of the five permanent members of the Security Council are not within the court's jurisdiction. The absence of these big states, along with India, means that despite the fact that a majority of UN members have accepted its jurisdiction, a majority of the world's population remains beyond its reach.

ARTICLE 1 OF THE STATUTE OF THE INTERNATIONAL CRIMINAL COURT

An International Criminal Court ('the Court') is hereby established. It shall be a permanent institution and shall have the power to exercise its jurisdiction over persons for the most serious crimes of international concern, as referred to in this Statute, and shall be complementary to national criminal jurisdictions.

In addition to this major problem of jurisdiction, the early days of the ICC were dogged by a series of controversies. Its first trial, of a warlord from the Democratic Republic of Congo, which should have had a major historical and symbolic importance, instead collapsed when the Court ruled that it had breached its own procedures. There were also sustained complaints from within the human rights community itself and beyond about the style and competence of its first chief prosecutor, Luis Moreno-Ocampo of Argentina. In particular, his announcement in 2008 that he intended to pursue the indictment of the president of Sudan on charges of genocide in Darfur was widely regarded as legally questionable and politically ill-judged.

Is the ICC project as a whole compromised by these shortcomings? On the fundamental test of its practical contribution to international justice the answer is probably no. However limited its jurisdiction, it has initiated a number of important processes since it began to function fully in 2005. Beyond the embarrassment over the Congo case, others have been pursued relating to events in Uganda and the Central African Republic. Certainly, the ICC has declined to initiate cases from the Iraq war on the grounds that while war crimes have plainly taken place there, those alleged against non-jurisdictional states (including, of course, the United States) have not been of sufficient seriousness to warrant investigation by the Court. Even if the ICC were determined to pursue citizens of non-jurisdictional states, its only recourse would be to refer the state in question to the Security Council; not an action likely to produce positive results in the case of one of the P5. But an inability to pursue all war criminals does not invalidate the pursuit of some war criminals. And the referral relationship between the ICC and the Security Council operates in both directions. The Council may refer any situation to the Court whether or not the alleged crimes relate to a state which has accepted jurisdiction. Sudan is not a jurisdictional state, but the Darfur investigation by the ICC was originally passed to it by the Security Council in 2005. There may be a certain queasiness about the Security Council, the majority of whose own permanent members do not themselves accept the Court's authority, acting in this way but, again, the perfect should not be an enemy of the possible.

The main point about the ICC, and a major thrust of the arguments for its creation, is that it will be permanent. The institution is in its infancy and the possibilities for its development – in terms of the expansion of its jurisdiction and the range of its legal remit – are considerable. Like the rest of the network of international humanitarian and rights law overseen by the United Nations, the ICC is a statement of aspiration as much as a legal instrument. The growth of its authority may prove painfully slow and incremental, and setbacks as well as advances may punctuate its development. The pace of legal advance will always be regulated by national and international political priorities. But the very existence of the ICC represents an important stage in the establishment and spread of international norms and the construction global governance. Its major contribution, therefore, is to mark a direction of travel towards, not world government perhaps, but at least more effective world governance.

Decolonization and development

Many founding ambitions of the United Nations in the fields of global peace, security and law were really developments on the model already created by the League of Nations. But in one important area – social and economic development – the UN built a major role for itself virtually from scratch. Interest in these fields had existed in the League, of course. The specialized agencies over which it provided an institutional umbrella, such as the International Labour Office and the Red Cross, existed to improve global social conditions. But issues of economic and social development were touched on only briefly in the League's Covenant which was otherwise preoccupied with the high politics of peace and security. In 1939 a League committee chaired by a former Australian prime minister, Stanley Bruce, did propose the creation of a permanent committee on social and economic affairs. Coming at the end of the organization's meaningful existence, however, the idea did not have a chance to develop. Yet the Bruce report anticipated one of the major departures of the UN. Chapter IX of the Charter (articles 55–60) deals with 'International Social and Economic Cooperation' while Chapter X outlines the powers and purposes of the Economic and Social Council (ECOSOC). When the UN was constructed, ECOSOC was marked out as one of its principal organs.

There were several reasons for this new emphasis on social and economic affairs under the UN. As the existence of the

Bruce Committee suggests, there had been a general move towards a greater focus on social development even before the outbreak of the Second World War. But the war itself and the unprecedented social and economic destruction it brought to the world made it inevitable that the new global organization would devote much greater attention to the challenges of social and economic reconstruction than its predecessor had done. Then, just as the immediate problems of post-war population displacement and social and economic repair began to recede, a larger global process gave a new emphasis to developmental problems. The worldwide and startlingly rapid process of decolonization utterly changed the nature of the international system in which the UN operated. The security problems of the post-colonial world and the UN's response to them have already been explored. But in reality, crises of economic and social development lay at the roots of most of these conflicts, civil and international, which challenged international peace and security.

Decolonization and self-determination

One of the most sacred purposes of the League of Nations, at least from the perspective of Woodrow Wilson's international morality, was the pursuit of national self-determination. Bringing political power into alignment with national cultural identities was considered by League enthusiasts as not merely being morally right, but as a precondition of a stable and secure world. For the League in the 1920s the main work in this regard was located in Europe. Three great continental empires – Hapsburg Austria, Hohenzollern Germany and Ottoman Turkey – were dismantled after 1918, creating new states in Central and Eastern Europe such as Czechoslovakia and Yugoslavia in the process. (Ironically, of course, neither of these survived the twentieth century because of demands for self-determination among their component parts.) Beyond this rather Eurocentric approach to the principle of self-determination, the League did begin to shift European attitudes to national rights elsewhere in the world as well through its mandate system. This treated the colonies beyond Europe of the powers defeated in the First World War as responsibilities of their new administering powers (appointed from among the victors) rather than as new possessions. In this way, European control of these territories was to be a preliminary to self-determination rather than a substitute for it (see Chapter 1).

As with other aspects of the League's work, when the UN took over the mandate system it sought to disguise a politically embarrassing continuity with a supposedly failed organization through a change in terminology. The Mandate Commission became the Trusteeship Council which, like the Economic and Social Council (ECOSOC), forms one of the six principal organs of the UN system. The trusteeship system has two entire chapters of the Charter, numbers XII and XIII, devoted to it but it is the one that precedes them that has had the highest political profile over the years. Chapter XI of the Charter takes the form of a 'Declaration Regarding Non-Self-Governing Territories'. The UN approach marked an advance of the League's position – which applied mandates only to the colonies of the defeated powers in the First World War – in that it deals with all 'territories whose peoples have not yet attained a full measure of self-government'. It therefore related to the colonies even of permanent members of the Security Council such as Britain and France, whose overseas empires were still vast in 1945. Those powers were now required to 'recognize the principle that the interests of the inhabitants of these territories are paramount, and accept as a sacred trust the obligation to promote to the utmost … the well-being of the inhabitants of these territories'.

Predictably, the Declaration was controversial when first formulated. The idea of adopting such a legalistic approach to colonialism was, unsurprisingly perhaps, an American one. Yet the original proposal was even more radical; it would have demanded a clear commitment from all imperial powers to bring their colonies to independence as quickly as possible. Both Britain and France reacted angrily to this. The French in particular had long regarded their colonies as integral parts of the nation for whom the concept of independence was philosophically meaningless. The big powers therefore agreed that the term 'independence' would be replaced by 'self-government' in the final Declaration. Still, once in place in the Charter, the Declaration represented an acceptance by the major imperial powers of an emerging new reality: colonial domination was now no longer accepted as a permanent feature of international politics.

This semantic compromise was just one retreat from a more radical view of the post-1945 world. Although the UN approach went further than that of the League by increasing the degree of international supervision of trust, in a crucial way the system eventually put in place fell well short of the high ambitions of President Roosevelt. His idea had been that the trusteeship arrangements should cover every colonial territory as of 1945 and not just the old League mandates over German and Turkish territories which had been distributed after the First World War. If the new approach had been adopted there would have been no British, French, Dutch, Portuguese or other empires but instead a series of UN administered trust territories embracing all existing colonies. The national obligation to prepare colonies for independence, which itself had proved unacceptable to Britain and France, would have been irrelevant under this arrangement. The UN as an institution would have determined the pace of decolonization everywhere. For the European victors of 1945 who were now permanent members of the Security Council this was simply unthinkable. Mandating the colonies of the defeated was one thing, expropriating the empires of the victors was quite another. The notion was particularly offensive to the great British imperialist, Winston Churchill, and the original more radical idea was quietly abandoned.

The power of the South

Whatever the retreat from the original vision, the UN's intervention in the vexed issue of empire, and its insistence on a role in the pace and character of decolonization, guaranteed it a key place in one of the most profoundly significant global processes of the twentieth century. The perception of the UN as an advocate of decolonization, along with its role as a welcoming home for the new states which emerged from the process, gave it a uniquely important place in the political and economic perspectives of the new global South. Sovereign equality in the General Assembly provided many new small states with a voice in world politics that they could never have hoped for otherwise.

The United Nations also provided a space, both political and physical, for South–South cooperation and for the pooling of national interests. From this base there emerged a variety of Third World organizations that added their own pressure for a final end to imperialism. A charismatic first generation of postcolonial leaders – Nehru of India, Nasser of Egypt, Nkrumah of Ghana – built the powerful Afro-Asian bloc in the General Assembly and then used it as a vehicle to make their individual and collective impact on world politics more generally. In the UN their principal achievement was probably the 'Declaration on the Granting of Independence to Colonial Countries and Peoples'. This was adopted as a resolution of the General

Assembly in December 1960. Effectively a development of the Charter's Declaration Regarding Non-Self-Governing Territories, the new statement of intent insisted, quite simply, 'that the process of liberation is irresistible and irreversible and that, in order to avoid serious crises, an end must be put to colonialism'.[12] The Declaration was passed by a massive majority with no opposing votes and only nine abstentions, mainly from the remaining imperial states of the time.

The political influence of the emerging global South probably reached its zenith in the 1970s, after which it gradually declined as the relative power of the General Assembly diminished against that of the Security Council. The greatest cause of this decline was not political, however. The waning of the South's influence was the result of hard economic and developmental realties. The failure of development in the South could not be permanently obscured by the political rhetoric of Third World leaders or the raw arithmetic of General Assembly membership. The main forum for the Third World in the UN at the time of the grouping's greatest influence was the Conference on Trade and Industry (UNCTAD). The first meeting of this was in Geneva in 1964, from which a group of seventy-seven Third World countries emerged with the mission of finding a common position in matters of trade and aid. The most celebrated achievement of the so-called 'Group of 77' was the New International Economic Order (NIEO). This was formulated at a Special Session of the UN General Assembly in April and May 1974. This was the year following the onset of the first oil crisis of the 1970s, which had a particularly hard impact on Third World countries. The NIEO consisted of a series of aspirations and targets which, if achieved, would have fundamentally changed the terms of North–South economic relations. It called for reduction of tariffs on the import of goods from the South into the North and for stabilization mechanisms which would prevent destructive swings in commodity prices.

The NIEO also called for the transfer of manufacturing technology from North to South to equalize the global balance of productive power. The principal proposal for development aid was that donor countries in the North should undertake to increase their economic support for the South to 0.7 of their gross national product.

The NIEO marked the high point of the South's influence in the UN. But it also illustrated the sharp limit that the states of the North were able to impose on this influence when they considered their own central interests to be threatened. Although the proposals were greeted publicly with statements of general sympathy, it soon became clear that there was no real chance of the NIEO becoming a reality in any significant sense. Quite simply, to put it in place would incur tangible costs for the North and ultimately there was no effective leverage at the South's disposal which would enable them to force the pace – whatever General Assembly resolutions they might engineer.

For the countries of the North it was the Bretton Woods institutions – in effect the World Bank and the International Monetary Fund – that were the proper vehicles for the regulation of the global economy. These institutions will be discussed in more detail shortly, but it was no coincidence that they were firmly under the control of the North. Henceforward this inescapable reality of power would shape the contribution of the United Nations to economic and social development. This contribution is by any measure a large one (the greater part of the UN's budget of around US$20 billion is devoted to it) and it is made through the existing Economic and Social Council. But by the beginning of the twenty-first century the influence of the Group of 77 – still in existence and still so-named, though now with upwards of 130 members – has declined dramatically from its high point. Similarly, its institutional launch pad, UNCTAD, which developed after 1964 into a permanent forum of the United Nations rather than a one-off gathering, continues to meet every four years. But while it provides some invaluable services, particularly in its collection and dissemination of statistical data, it has an ever diminishing influence on the workings of the real global economy.

The UN and the Bretton Woods institutions

Reflecting the hard reality of economic power in the world, the influence which has slipped away from the Group of 77 now lies unequivocally in the hands of the so-called Bretton Woods institutions. These are more or less wholly controlled by the developed North. While the architects of the United Nations were sitting down together at Dumbarton Oaks in 1944, a similarly leafy location was the scene of a parallel piece of post-war planning. This other project was designed to reorder the regulation not of global peace and security but of the world economy. The gathering was held in the New Hampshire town of Bretton Woods. Forty-four allied countries, including the Soviet Union, were represented there. The most significant outcome was the establishment of permanent organizations (the first Bretton Woods institutions), most importantly the International Bank for Reconstruction and Development (IBRD), which became known as the World Bank, and the International Monetary Fund (IMF). The immediate concern of the meeting was the prospects for post-war reconstruction given that in July 1944, the defeat of the Axis powers seemed inevitable. Underlying this though was the memory of the pre-war global depression which had inflicted enormous damage on every country represented at the meeting. The national delegates at Bretton Woods were determined that the new world economy would be regulated in a way which would prevent such a catastrophe recurring – just as post-war world politics were to be regulated by the United Nations to prevent the catastrophe of another world war.

The guiding principle of the Bretton Woods institutions would be the pursuit of global free trade. To this end, the first priority was the stabilization of the post-war global economic system. The World Bank was intended originally to provide long term and secure loans to countries in urgent need of support in the process of post-war reconstruction. Simultaneously, the IMF was designed to carry out the parallel function of stabilizing national currencies and the exchange rates between them in order to encourage and maintain effective global trade. But as post-war reconstruction neared completion in the late 1950s and early 1960s, the world economy was confronted by a new set of challenges. The comprehensive process of decolonization brought into the international state system a wave of new states with fragile national finances and only a very weak presence in the global economy. At this point, then, the focus of the World Bank and the IMF shifted from parts of the world which had sought to recover their economic health after the war to those which had never had a healthy economic position to regain. The most important role of the World Bank now was to provide loans for specific development projects, for the most part large scale infrastructural ones in the global South. The task of the IMF was to secure the required national economic base from which those projects could be launched and so reduce the risk to the Bank's investments.

The relationship between the Bretton Woods institutions and the United Nations is complex – and also frequently difficult. Formally, the World Bank and the IMF are part of the United Nations system as specialized agencies. In reality, though, they have a much higher level of autonomy than other such institutions. They are governed by their own constitutions rather than the Charter and they do business directly with governments and not through the channel of the General

Assembly or the Economic and Social Council. Most controversially, perhaps, their formal structure gives a dominant role to the developed capitalist countries of the West (the chairman of the World Bank, for example, is by custom always an American). Their pursuit of fiscal discipline and convertible national currencies as prerequisites to free trade has often brought them into conflict with what might be called the development community. These experts and organizations, many of them within the UN system, exist as advocates for increased equity between North and South through the creation of a fairer global economic system in which the interests of the weakest players are given special protection. This grinds against the neoliberal, market-orientated philosophy which has prevailed in the IMF and World Bank since the 1980s (and particularly since the collapse of Communism). The Bretton Woods institutions, with their sometimes evangelical commitment to the free play of market forces in the world economy, have been accused of imposing 'turbo-capitalism' on the world.

The frontline of this battle has been located around the Structural Adjustment Programmes (SAPs) – or 'conditionalities' – which are set as the necessary price for World Bank and IMF loans and support to enfeebled national economies. Typically, SAPs involve the privatization of state enterprises and services, reductions in state-provided public services and the removal of national protectionism in trade. This hard medicine is purportedly designed to prepare countries seeking support to become effective actors in the largely unregulated globalized economy. Ultimately, their advocates argue, SAPs are the most effective route to poverty reduction and sustainable development. This has not always been evident at the local level, however. As many post-colonial economies in the South are built around state-owned or state-controlled enterprises, rapid, externally driven privatization tends to generate huge wealth for a few individuals at the expense of the nation as a whole. Also, in many countries of the South the public sector is the main source of employment – from the higher levels of the civil service to the least skilled manual jobs. The requirement in SAPs to roll-back this state involvement has led to considerable hardship in many already desperately poor countries. Moreover, local livelihoods have also been lost through the enforced removal of trade protectionism which has opened up markets to imports from large foreign manufacturers with which local producers and providers simply cannot compete. And, the complaint is often heard, while imports to the South are increasingly liberalized, there is often no reciprocity from the North where import controls on goods manufactured in the South still operate. Additionally, while these manufactured products from the South may be locked out of markets in the North, the governments of developed countries will often subsidize their own farm production (for example through the European Union's agricultural policies) so that even primary, non-manufactured produce from the South cannot compete. This can affect not only the South's penetration of markets in the North but their control of their own – non-subsidized – markets in the face of exports from the North.

Not surprisingly, the Bretton Woods institutions have coexisted very uneasily with influential voices in the UN General Assembly where the global South remains strongly represented. The wishes of the General Assembly, though, are easily over-ridden in any confrontation with the sharp-edged forces of economic globalization in which neoliberal prescriptions are the favoured remedy of the most powerful actors. In recent years, however, there have been some signs that the Bretton Woods institutions themselves are questioning the long term utility of their own SAPs. Moreover, since the formulation of the UN's Millennium Development Goals in 2000, the IMF and the World Bank have been constrained to work within the framework of new and specific poverty reduction targets. To this extent at least, the UN has managed to rein-in the more fundamentalist free-market instincts that had been in play for the previous two decades. For many countries, however, this more nuanced approach has come too late to prevent the social and economic dislocation wrought by SAPs forced on them in the 1980s and 1990s.

ECOSOC and the specialized agencies

The Economic and Social Council (ECOSOC), established at the outset in 1945 as one of the principal organs of the UN, serves as the coordinating body for the organization's developmental activities and the principal forum for their discussion. ECOSOC's work reflects the changing priorities which have emerged over the life of the UN. Initially occupied mainly with post-war reconstruction in Europe, with decolonization in the 1950s and 1960s its attention turned to problems of underdevelopment among the new members of the UN. The Council has fifty-four members elected by the General Assembly for three-year terms which overlap to guarantee continuity. Places are distributed on a geographical basis: fourteen going to Africa, eleven to Asia, thirteen to Western Europe and North America, six to Eastern Europe and ten to Latin America and the Caribbean. The Council, which is based at the UN's Geneva headquarters, meets in a four week session involving its full membership annually, with other meetings held as and when necessary. Historically, though, much of ECOSOC's work has been carried out through its five Regional Commissions: for Europe, Latin America and the Caribbean, Africa, Western Asia and the Pacific. More recently ECOSOC has tended to work through specialized agencies with specific functions, both from within the UN system and from

the non-governmental community, on issues of global significance rather than on the basis of the regional Commissions.
These organizations range from the large and powerful Bretton
Woods institutions we have just discussed to much smaller
and narrowly focused ones dealing with everything from
climate to postal communications. ECOSOC also liaises closely
with other related UN headquarter bodies such as the
High Commission for Refugees and the Department for
Peacekeeping Operations.

UN DEVELOPMENT RELATED SPECIALIZED AGENCIES

Food and Agriculture Organization (FAO)
International Fund for Agricultural Development (IFAD)
International Labour Organization (ILO)
International Monetary Fund (IMF)
International Narcotics Control Board (INCB)
United Nations Children's Fund (UNICEF)
United Nations Development Programme (UNDP)
United Nations Educational, Scientific and Cultural Organization
(UNESCO)
United Nations Industrial Development Organization (UNIDO)
World Bank Group
World Health Organization (WHO)
World Tourism Organization

Many of the specialized agencies of which ECOSOC has
oversight are venerable institutions in their own right, having
been in existence consistently (or with only minor changes of
name) since the beginning of the twentieth century. The
International Labour Organization (originally Office) and the
Universal Postal Union are among a number of bodies which

had previously operated within the League of Nations system. Meanwhile others, such as the International Atomic Energy Authority and the World Tourism Organization, exist to deal with uniquely modern concerns.

Among the most important hands-on funds and programmes under the ECOSOC umbrella are the Food and Agriculture Organization (FAO), the Children's Fund (UNICEF) and the Development Programme (UNDP). The FAO, at least in terms of personnel and offices, is the largest of the specialized agencies in the UN system, which is perhaps appropriate given the scale of its task: some 800 million people worldwide live without adequate food. Its primary roles are to alleviate hunger and to improve nutrition through the provision of project aid and research resources. A World Food Summit held in the FAO's headquarters in Rome in 1996 set long term priorities for the Organization within a context of sustainable development (this was set out in the Rome Declaration). Within a very few years, however, the world encountered a crisis in food production and distribution which looked as if it would set a major part of the development agenda for the twenty-first century. This was brought on by a range of factors from environmental change to increased world demand from the new surging economies of China and India. Suddenly and unexpectedly food security has become one of the greatest challenges to the UN's economic and social efforts for the twenty-first century.

The Children's Fund, UNICEF, is another of the largest specialized agencies. UNICEF is concerned with the provision of minimal standards of nutrition, primary health care and basic education among the ever growing numbers of children in the world population. Like many other UN agencies, UNICEF was originally established (in 1946) to confront the massive post-war problems of Europe and Asia, in particular that of war orphans and displaced children. When this ceased to be a

Figure 7 UN Food Aid, Democratic Republic of Congo (UN Photo by Marie Frechon)

major task, UNICEF's attentions shifted to the emerging problems of underdevelopment in the global South. Here too its priorities, like those of most of the specialized agencies, have shifted over the years as different challenges have come and, occasionally, gone. Since the 1980s its health programmes have increasingly involved the consequences of mother-to-child transmission of HIV/AIDS. Much more than in the past, too, UNICEF has had to concern itself with the protection of children from violence and exploitation. One of UNICEF's landmark achievements in this area was the adoption by the General Assembly of the Convention on the Rights of the Child in 1989.

The United Nations Development Programme has a wider brief than either the FAO or UNICEF, though the work of all three agencies frequently overlaps, a fact which underlines the importance of ECOSOC as a coordinating body. Created by the General Assembly in the mid-1960s just as the rhythm of decolonization was at its fastest, the UNDP manages the greater part of the UN's socio-economic projects in the South. Like that of UNICEF, the focus of the UNDP's work has shifted over the years, reflecting changing development priorities. Its original objectives – poverty reduction through income generating projects, job creation and increasing literacy by working closely with national governments – remain in place. But increasingly it has approached these goals in the context of gender equality and environmental protection. It has also created a network of programmes addressing the threat of HIV/AIDS. Its white 4x4s have become a ubiquitous feature of the streetscapes of towns and cities throughout the tropics.

Since 1990 the UNDP has raised awareness of development issues worldwide through its annual Human Development Index (HDI). Each year it ranks almost every country in the world according to a set of development criteria (per capita income, infant mortality, literacy rates etc.) and produces a graded list. In 2007–2008, for example, Iceland came top and Sierra Leone bottom of the 177 countries measured. Perhaps unsurprisingly, sub-Saharan Africa occupied all twenty-seven lowest positions. Movement within the HDI from year to year is a generally reliable indicator of a country's success in poverty alleviation. The annual budget of the UNDP – covering expenditure on projects in more than 160 countries – is over US$4 billion, the greater part of which is drawn from voluntary contributions by UN member states.

The FAO, UNICEF and the UNDP exist primarily to contribute to the longer term processes of development in the South. While they have a role in the provision of emergency and disaster aid, this area of the UN's work has generated its own agencies and systems. This has been a necessary development as the demand for such emergency intervention rose

UNDP HUMAN DEVELOPMENT INDEX, 2007–2008

Top 20	Bottom 20
1 Iceland	158 Nigeria
2 Norway	159 Tanzania
3 Australia	160 Guinea
4 Canada	161 Rwanda
5 Ireland	162 Angola
6 Sweden	163 Benin
7 Switzerland	164 Malawi
8 Japan	165 Zambia
9 Netherlands	166 Côte d'Ivoire
10 France	167 Burundi
11 Finland	168 Dem. Rep. of Congo
12 United States	169 Ethiopia
13 Spain	170 Chad
14 Denmark	171 Central African Republic
15 Austria	172 Mozambique
16 United Kingdom	173 Mali
17 Belgium	174 Niger
18 Luxembourg	175 Guinea-Bissau
19 New Zealand	176 Burkina Faso
20 Italy	177 Sierra Leone

dramatically in the last years of the twentieth century. The post-Cold War years were marked by destructive local conflicts from South Asia to West Africa and from the Middle East to the Caribbean with the most awful humanitarian consequences. Additionally, climate change has increased the number and severity of many natural disasters which also require coordinated multilateral responses.

Probably the most high profile UN agency at work in situations of man-made crisis is the High Commission for Refugees (UNHCR). Like ECOSOC itself and many other bodies it oversees such as UNICEF, the UNHCR emerged from the setting of post-Second World War reconstruction and changed its focus to meet the new priorities. The new focus was determined initially by the fall-out from peripheral conflicts during the Cold War and later by the plague of post-Cold War civil and regional wars. The formal definition of refugee status in international law relates only to individuals seeking refuge across national borders, but the nature of much contemporary conflict means that the UNHCR is as often involved in aiding the millions of internally displaced persons (IDPs) who have been forced by conflicts in one part of their country to seek safety elsewhere inside its borders. In the first years of the twenty-first century the UNHCR was supporting more than forty million people across the world, divided roughly equally between international refugees and IDPs.

THE 'REFUGEE' DEFINED: THE 1951 UNITED NATIONS CONVENTION RELATING TO THE STATUS OF REFUGEES

A refugee is an individual who:
owing to well-founded fear of being persecuted for reasons of race, religion, nationality, membership of a particular social group or political opinion, is outside the country of his nationality and is unable, or owing to such fear, is unwilling to avail himself of the protection of that country; or who, not having a nationality and being outside the country of his former habitual residence as a result of such events, is unable or, owing to such fear, is unwilling to return to it.

Since the late 1990s the UNHCR, other UN agencies and many non-UN bodies as well have responded to complex emergencies under the organizational umbrella of the United Nations Office for the Coordination of Humanitarian Affairs (OCHA). This was formed originally by the General Assembly, to which it reports directly, in 1991 to replace the Office of the Disaster Relief Coordinator. OCHA was designed to meet two new needs. First, it was a response to the growing demands for coordinated humanitarian relief, particularly as a result of conflict. But it also provided a structure which could manage the growing number of non-governmental organizations (NGOs) which have become involved in relief operations. Duplication of effort, misuse of limited resources and, frequently, inter-agency conflicts were becoming more and more common and the need for a single coordinating body was becoming urgent. The authority and status of OCHA is reinforced by its high position within the structures of the United Nations as a department parallel to that of Peacekeeping Operations and Political Affairs. As such, it is headed by its own under-secretary-general.

The Monterrey Consensus and the Millennium Development Goals

During the 1990s there was a net fall in the amount of development aid directed through the UN and other agencies to the global South (see textbox). Between 1994 and 1997 alone the total amount of support given by governments in the developed North to the poorest countries diminished by about US$10 billion. It was perhaps no coincidence that this drop followed the end of the Cold War and the end of the competition between East and West for friends in the South. In 2002 a major UN conference was held in Monterrey in Mexico at which both donors and recipients of aid were represented. From this emerged the Monterrey Consensus which attempted to set out responsibilities for both sides in the aid relationship. The North was called on to reverse the slippage in the assistance it transferred to the South and to accept fixed commitments to specific contributions. The countries of the South, for their part, were to increase efforts to improve the quality of their governance and of their national management of aid and development. This was to be done by increasing administrative efficiency and stamping down on corruption. Following Monterrey, levels of development assistance began to increase once again.

WORLD DEVELOPMENT AID FLOWS 2002–2007

(Based on OECD data)

Year	Total US$m
1992	68,292
1993	61,570
1994	64,925
1995	65,133
1996	62,153
1997	54,890
1998	58,264
1999	59,195
2000	59,790
2001	59,578
2002	58,297
2003	79,674
2004	91,847
2005	120,373
2006	119,780
2007	120,682

The Monterrey discussions, and the subsequent increase in aid transfers, derived in large part from the establishment of the

United Nations Millennium Development Goals (MDGs) two years previously (see textbox). This landmark statement of development aspirations has come to shape the priorities of the various ECOSOC agencies, particularly UNICEF and the UNDP. The Millennium Development Goals were set out by the then secretary-general, Kofi Annan, in an attempt to appropriate the symbolism of the calendar to reinvigorate commitment in the North to the social and economic development of the South. This commitment, strong at least at a rhetorical level in the 1960s and 1970s, had by the end of the century fallen away to the point where some areas of the world, particularly in sub-Saharan Africa, were actually becoming more rather than less underdeveloped. The eight stark goals set out in the MDGs, supposedly to be realized by 2015, provide a distillation of the world's social and economic priorities at the beginning of the twenty-first century. Their pursuit is perhaps the most critical task currently facing the United Nations. The aims, each of which comes with specific targets, cover poverty eradication, primary education, gender equality, child mortality, maternal health, the fight against malaria and HIV/AIDS, environmental sustainability and the terms of the North–South partnership for development. If achieved the MDGs will be a more significant contribution by the UN system to global well-being than anything relating to the rule of international law or even peace-keeping that we have already explored. It soon became clear that the prospects for meeting the goals by 2015 were far from certain, however.

In July 2007, at the opening of the annual ECOSOC session in Geneva, Secretary-General Ban Ki-moon introduced a much anticipated half-time report on the advance towards the goals. Mid-way through the process, the signs for success were, to say the least, mixed. On poverty reduction, the power of the Chinese and Indian economies had made the minimum income target (bringing down the proportion of those living on less than

THE UNITED NATIONS MILLENNIUM DEVELOPMENT GOALS

Goal 1. Eradicate extreme poverty and hunger

Halve, between 1990 and 2015, the proportion of people whose income is less than one dollar a day.

Halve, between 1990 and 2015, the proportion of people who suffer from hunger.

Goal 2. Achieve universal primary education

Ensure that, by 2015, children everywhere, boys and girls alike, will be able to complete a full course of primary schooling.

Goal 3. Promote gender equality and empower women

Eliminate gender disparity in primary and secondary education, preferably by 2005, and to all levels of education no later than 2015.

Goal 4. Reduce child mortality

Reduce by two-thirds, between 1990 and 2015, the under-five mortality rate.

Goal 5. Improve maternal health

Reduce by three-quarters, between 1990 and 2015, the maternal mortality ratio.

Goal 6. Combat HIV/AIDS, malaria and other diseases

Have halted by 2015 and begun to reverse the spread of HIV/AIDS.

Have halted by 2015 and begun to reverse the incidence of malaria and other major diseases.

Goal 7. Ensure environmental sustainability

Integrate the principles of sustainable development into country policies and programmes and reverse the losses of environmental resources.

> ## THE UNITED NATIONS MILLENNIUM
> ## DEVELOPMENT GOALS (*cont.*)
>
> Halve by 2015 the proportion of people without sustainable access to safe drinking water.
> By 2020 to have achieved a significant improvement in the lives of at least 100 million slum dwellers.
>
> **Goal 8. Develop a Global Partnership for Development**
>
> Develop further an open, rule-based, predictable, non-discriminatory trading and financial system.
> Address the special needs of the least developed countries.
> Address the special needs of landlocked countries and small island developing States.
> Deal comprehensively with the debt problems of developing countries through national and international measures in order to make debt sustainable in the long term.
> In cooperation with developing countries, develop and implement strategies for decent and productive work for youth.
> In cooperation with pharmaceutical companies, provide access to affordable essential drugs in developing countries.
> In cooperation with the private sector, make available the benefits of new technologies, especially information and communications.

one US dollar day) achievable in two of the world's most populous countries. But there seemed little prospect of such success in sub-Saharan Africa. A similar situation exists in relation to the attack on hunger. While Asia is likely to achieve the target set for child size and health (the technical yardstick set), Africa is likely to fall short to the extent of some thirty million children. Paradoxically, the increased wealth which has increased food consumption in Asia has caused a demand-led increase in food prices which makes the prospect of hunger alleviation in Africa even more distant.

The feasibility of the goal of universal primary education was less easy to assess, but at the half-way point in the process twelve per cent of the age group worldwide were not at school. Again, Africa had the greatest problems with thirty per cent of children out of formal education. The central target for gender equality is itself related to education: an end to the disparity in the numbers of boys and girls at school. While there had been some success here on a global level, once again this tended to disguise serious failings regionally, particularly in Africa and South Asia.

KOFI ANNAN, *IN LARGER FREEDOM* (2005)

Progress in achieving the Millennium Development Goals has been far from uniform across the world. The greatest improvements have been in East Asia and South Asia, where more than 200 million people have been lifted out of poverty since 1990 alone. Nonetheless, nearly 700 million people in Asia still live on less than $1 a day – nearly two thirds of the world's poorest people – while even some of the fastest-growing countries are falling short on non-income Goals, such as protecting the environment and reducing maternal mortality. Sub-Saharan Africa is at the epicentre of the crisis, falling seriously short on most Goals, with continuing food insecurity, disturbingly high child and maternal mortality, growing numbers of people living in slums and an overall rise of extreme poverty despite some important progress in individual countries. Latin America, the transition economies, and the Middle East and North Africa, often hampered by growing inequality, have more mixed records, with significant variations in progress but general trends falling short of what is needed to meet the 2015 deadline.

On health, the goal of reducing maternal and infant mortality was far off-target at the mid-point in the process, with Africa again falling further behind other regions. The disease reduction goal showed a similar pattern. AIDS infection had risen globally by a factor of six between 2001 and 2007, though there was some sign that the rate of increase was levelling off. The situation with other diseases was worse. Malaria, despite clear public health advances, still killed about a million people each year worldwide, eighty per cent of them African children under five. The targets for sanitation and public health attached to the sustainable environmental goal are probably the ones that will be furthest from being achieved by 2015. The number of people without regular access to clean drinking water was to be halved according to the MDGs. Figures for 2004, however, showed that 2.6 billion people – nearly half the population of the world – had no such access and it was almost impossible that the massive reduction in this set by the Goals could come anywhere near being met.

Inevitably, perhaps, the manifest problems in the pursuit of the Millennium Development Goals and the likelihood that they will not be achieved is seen by many as yet more proof of the shortcomings of the United Nations. To the extent that the MDGs when set represented a victory of aspiration over experience, this is perhaps true – but only to that extent. In an international system of sovereign states the prospects for global development, just as much as those for peace and security and the rule of law, are ultimately an issue of political will within and between those states. The UN can provide a coordinating body along with the technical expertise to formulate and implement programmes – and over the years it has proved adept at doing so and in adapting to changing circumstances. But it cannot dictate national policies or the nature of the relationship between those giving and those receiving development assistance. Here as elsewhere the question should not be, why do UN projects so often fall short of their ambition? More properly, it should be simply: would we live in a better world without them, however constrained and imperfect their contribution might be?

7

Environment: sustainability and the future of the planet

It is not by accident that one of the UN Millennium Development Goals is concerned with the relationship between economic and social development issues and those of the environment. Goal 7 is to 'integrate the principles of sustainable development into country policies and programmes and reverse the losses of environmental resources'. Over recent years concerns about the world's physical environment have increasingly become intertwined with questions of human development. Global concern with the environment is itself a relatively recent phenomenon. The word environment does not appear in the United Nations Charter, nor would anyone in 1945 have expected it to. The idea of worldwide environmental risk let alone potential catastrophe was, quite literally, the stuff of science fiction even into the 1960s. When awareness of threats began to emerge, however, the United Nations was quick to respond and has, at least since the early 1970s, provided real leadership in the area. This, of course, is how it should be. The greatest environmental challenges are by their very nature global and transnational, and they can only be effectively met by coordinated action.

Yet this essential coordination in the face of environmental challenge is burdened with some special difficulties. Although this is an area where the acceptance of interdependence is essential if reciprocal benefits are to be achieved, it is also one where it is very difficult to build collective motivation and unity of purpose. For one thing, it is possible – and politically tempting – for countries simply to stand aside from generally agreed collective measures and leave the effort and pain of restoring and protecting environmental stability to everyone else. Once achieved, the communal benefits that come as a result of that effort and pain can still be enjoyed. Concerns over national image and prestige on the international stage which often drive compliance with other areas of international regulation can be overpowered by domestic pressure to protect particular industries in order to maintain established standards of living and lifestyles.

The consistent refusal by the United States over many years and under various presidencies to accept limits on the creation of greenhouse gases is only the most obvious example of this. A global community of mutual environmental concern is difficult to mobilize when it is composed of vastly different sets of expectations and traditions. For example, energy conservation policies that would require major domestic sacrifices in North American or European countries might hardly be noticed in sub-Saharan Africa or Southeast Asia. By definition the industrialized North will produce more pollution than the underdeveloped South and therefore should perhaps be expected to bear the greatest burden in correcting the damage this causes. But against this it can be argued that the North provides the benefits of its industries to those – less polluting – parts of the world which have no comparable industries of their own. It is an extremely difficult area in which to build a sense of global community, therefore. But it is one in which a collective approach is absolutely essential. This paradox is reflected in the mixed results achieved by the United Nations over the past three or four decades.

**KOFI ANNAN ON THE ENVIRONMENT
(MILLENNIUM REPORT TO THE GENERAL
ASSEMBLY, 2000)**

The founders of the UN set out in the words of the Charter; to promote social progress and better standards of life in larger freedom – above all, freedom from want and freedom from fear. In 1945, they could not have anticipated, however, the urgent need we face today to realize yet a third: the freedom of future generations to sustain their lives on this planet. We are failing to provide it. On the contrary, we have been plundering our children's future heritage to pay for environmentally unsustainable practices.

The early environment conferences

The first major intervention by the United Nations in the area of the physical as opposed to the political and economic world came in 1972 with the Stockholm Conference on the Human Environment. The original initiative for this came from the Swedish government (which was to be the host for the eventual gathering) which won General Assembly support for the project in 1968. It did so against opposition from other Western governments. Today the idea of the environment as an urgent area of concern is an obvious given. In the 1960s, however, it was still regarded by many as a vague and ill-defined side-issue of interest only to middle class liberals (and Sweden was easily caricatured as this tribe's natural home). Environmental issues, opponents argued, should more properly be dealt with by existing sectoral bodies in the UN system, such as ECOSOC, or by the specialized agencies.

However, the new prophets of environmental concern in the UN prevailed and the conference took place in June 1972 under

Canadian chairmanship. A total of 113 UN member states met in Stockholm. These included Communist China which had only recently been admitted to the UN and to permanent membership of the Security Council (see Chapter 2). In common with all large scale UN conferences, Stockholm unveiled its own Declaration composed of rather grandiose intentions. In fact, its main contribution was the raising of public awareness of the environment as a pressing global concern rather than the implementation of concrete policies. In the wake of Stockholm about a hundred governments created new environmental ministries or agencies. The conference also helped to establish the enduring connection in the UN's subsequent efforts between the physical environment and social and economic development. This critical connection was aided by an impassioned contribution to the plenary session by the Indian prime minister, Indira Gandhi, who was the only head of government present apart from the host, Olof Palme. 'Are not poverty and need', she demanded, 'the greatest polluters?'[13]

In organizational terms, a major outcome of Stockholm was the creation of the United Nations Environment Programme (UNEP). Originally established to drive the implementation of the Declaration and the accompanying Action Plan, UNEP quickly became the key UN agency for environmental protection and regulation. It has its headquarters in Nairobi, making it the only significant part of the central UN system to be located in sub-Saharan Africa. It is not a specialized agency, but a 'programme' of the United Nations, a subsidiary organ of the General Assembly comparable to the UN Development Programme. However, it differs in one important respect from the UNDP in that it is fully funded from the UN's regular budget rather than members' contributions. This funding amounts to about US$100 million annually. Its principal roles are to advise UN member countries on environmental issues and to assess and promote developments in international environmental law. UNEP is directed by a council of fifty-eight UN member states elected for four-year terms on a rolling basis. It publishes an annual report, the *Global Environmental Outlook*, which provides the definitive assessment of changes to the world's physical condition.

Twenty years after the groundbreaking Stockholm gathering, in a world dramatically changed both politically and environmentally, the UN held its next major conference, again convened by the General Assembly. This was what became known as the Earth Summit – formally, the United Nations Conference on the Environment and Development – which took place in Rio de Janeiro in June 1992. In the two decades between Stockholm and Rio public attitudes to the environment had changed utterly. By 1992 there was no question that the global environment was a pressing issue demanding collective action among states. It was now much more than a preoccupation for pressure groups in the West. The end of the Cold War was still relatively recent and the contemporary rhetoric of a new cooperative world order raised public expectations that the Earth Summit could mark a fundamental departure in the way the political world addressed its environmental responsibilities. In all, 178 UN member states gathered for the conference where they were lobbied and lectured by about 1400 nongovernmental organizations.

The initial outcomes of Rio were encouraging. The Rio Declaration, like its predecessor from Stockholm, stressed that the nurturing and protection of the physical environment was not a block to social and economic development. It also emphasized the need for the environment to become a bottom-up, grassroots concern and not just one for governments. In addition, two important legal conventions were opened for signature. These were the Convention on Biological Diversity (CBD) and the Framework Convention on Climate Control (UNFCCC). The first committed its signatories to the protection of biodiversity and action against the depletion of animal and plant species. The second was the first serious attempt to address the then still novel threat of man-made climate change. The Framework involved national commitments to the control and reduction of greenhouse gas emissions. It set the foundations of the Kyoto Protocol five years later (see below).

Beyond this, the most important statements to emerge from the Rio conference were what became known as Agenda 21: the *Agenda for Sustainable Development into the 21st Century*. A massive document of more than 800 pages, Agenda 21 ranges over the spectrum of environmental and environment related issues from pollution to biodiversity, deforestation to population and poverty to energy. Giving substance to the Rio Declaration's emphasis on bottom-up activity, the responsibility for the implementation of Agenda 21 reached down to the level of local government and interest groups (its familiar slogan is 'think global, act local').

The venue for the next major UN conference was Johannesburg in 2002, ten years after Rio. The main purpose of this conference was not so much to produce new initiatives or open new areas for regulation but to take stock of the situation after the Earth Summit and to assess the extent to which the varied and far-reaching initiatives begun there were being implemented. (For this reason Johannesburg has been described as Rio-plus-10.) Nevertheless, Johannesburg maintained the upward movement in the number of participants, both national and informal. One hundred and ninety-one states were represented there, along with no less than 8000 non-governmental organizations. This spectacular tally of NGOs was an indication of the astonishing growth of public interest in environmental issues. Johannesburg also came two years after the setting of the Millennium Development Goals and this was reflected in the focus of its discussions. The inevitable Johannesburg Action Plan (or Plan of Implementation) drawn up at the end of the conference gave as much prominence to poverty and hunger, health and basic education as it did to the more narrowly focused issues of the physical environment such as marine protection and the future of rain forests. By the time of Johannesburg the relationship between the environment and social and economic development, which had made its first tentative entry into the narrative three decades earlier at Stockholm, was unquestionable and unquestioned. The close inter-relationship between, for example, clean water and human development or between food security and respect for the land was now taken for granted.

The United Nations and the politics of climate change

Secretary-General Ban Ki-moon, speaking in November 2007, described climate change as the defining challenge of the age. By climate change, of course, he was referring to the phenomenon of global warming. This, the weight of serious scientific thinking now agrees, is caused primarily by the long term increase in the emission of so-called greenhouse gases among which the greatest offender is carbon dioxide (CO_2). Produced by the industrial and domestic use of fossil fuels such as oil and coal, world CO_2 emissions should in principle be controllable by international agreement. The result of the current rate of warming is a likely increase in mean global temperatures of anything from 1.4 to 5.8 degrees centigrade by the year 2100. This brings in its tail the melting of the polar icecaps and consequent rapid rises in sea levels. It will also cause desertification of huge swathes of currently productive land as well as the loss of essential biodiversity with all the catastrophic human disasters that will follow. The combination of apocalyptic global threat and the necessity of transnational action to meet it, gives the

United Nations an inescapable leadership responsibility in the attempt to reach a viable solution.

The frightening extent of this threat to the world's common future emerged during the 1990s. Previously, the main focus for unified action on global climate had been damage to the ozone layer recorded by scientists in the 1970s. This layer of the Earth's atmosphere filters out most of the dangerous ultraviolet rays which approach from space and which, if not deflected in this way, would pose a major threat to animal and plant life. Here too, the problem appeared to be man-made, a product of contemporary domestic and industrial activities. The ozone layer, it appeared, was being destroyed by the rapid increase in the use of chlorofluorocarbons (CFCs) which were widely used in aerosol sprays and in refrigeration. The UN Environment Programme had been active in confronting the problem and in warning of the risks of CFC use since the mid-1970s, but only Sweden, leading the field here as in other areas of environmental protection, unilaterally banned their use (in 1978). The situation worldwide changed only in the mid-1980s when the unexpected extent of the depletion of the ozone layer over Antarctica was measured and the urgency of the threat to the global environment fully realized. UNEP was now in a position to push for multilateral action.

The Montreal Protocol on Substances that Deplete the Ozone Layer, which was opened for signature in 1989, committed countries signing up to it to the virtual elimination of the manufacture and use of CFCs by the end of the 1990s. The Montreal process was the product of extremely delicate negotiations which highlighted some of the recurring difficulties which can hinder the establishment of fair global environmental regulation. In many countries of the South, where personal aerosols were not as widely used and domestic refrigeration still a luxury, the CFC problem was often seen as one created by a recklessly consumerist North. To deal with the problem, however, the South was expected to constrain its own social and economic development. There was also a fear that countries in the South would be used as dumping grounds for obsolete CFC-using products and processes from the North as countries there moved on to new, less damaging technologies. In the event, these concerns were overcome and the Montreal Protocol (with a series of subsequent updates and a total signature list of 166 countries) seems to have been a success. Periodic remeasurements of the Antarctic ozone layer appear to show the hole repairing itself.

This apparent quick and easy success for global environmental regulation had the understandable but unhelpful effect of raising misguided expectations that the next global challenge, that of greenhouse gas emissions and global warming, could be as easily solved. This was not to be the case. For one thing, the chemical industry quickly found a straightforward substitute for CFC. As the Montreal process gained momentum CFCs gave way to HFCs (hydrofluorocarbons) which had similar qualities (though ironically HFCs are themselves greenhouse gases, albeit minor in their impact compared to CO_2). Even in the absence of an immediate substitute for CFCs, aerosol sprays and refrigeration gases play relatively minor roles in the world's daily life and, in extremis, steps could have been taken to control them without major disruption. Global warming and its man-made causes are of a totally different order, however. Fossil fuels quite literally drive the world; virtually all global industry and transport is dependent on them. And by the beginning of the twenty-first century the problem was set to increase dramatically with the rapid industrial (and social) development of both China and India. One often quoted statistic suggests that China is currently opening a new coal-fired power station every week.

In 1988 the UN established its Intergovernmental Panel on Climate Change (IPCC). Formed as a joint venture between UNEP and the World Meteorological Organization (WMO), itself a UN specialized agency, the Panel was to provide objective scientific information in an area which from the outset was highly contentious. There were those who denied the very existence of climate change. When scientific data made this climate change denial untenable, the debate shifted away from the fact of rising temperatures to their cause. Supposedly natural reasons for change, such as solar activity or simple historical oscillations in temperatures were advanced by those who, for whatever reasons, were unhappy with the idea that climate change was due to the burning of fossil fuels. Many vested interests were involved. Initially the major oil companies were, for obvious reasons, at the forefront of scepticism about the role of their products. Other industries that feared regulation would affect their productivity joined in. Similarly, there were many – especially right-wing – commentators who were just temperamentally hostile to what they saw as another liberal environmentalist panic story. The IPCC has been instrumental in shifting the discussion on from these early, unproductive brawls and in making the fact of man-made climate change a given in all serious debates about regulation. This does not mean, however, that effective climate change regulation has followed.

The IPCC's first major report, published in 1990, shaped the agenda of the Rio Earth Summit two years later. There, as we have seen, the UNFCCC was opened for signature. This committed its signatories to the 'stabilization of greenhouse gas concentrations in the atmosphere at a level that would prevent dangerous anthropogenic interference with the climate system'. The UNFCCC was accepted by a total of 154 countries. But while it was an important symbolic advance, it did not impose any very specific obligations. These were to be elaborated at a subsequent meeting which would be held in Kyoto in Japan in December 1997. It was here, when clear and unequivocal commitments to action with national policy implications were required, that the fundamental international division over climate change and what to do about it became brutally clear.

The Kyoto Protocol to the United Nations Framework Convention on Climate Change, to give it its full title, was opened for signature in March 1998, setting concrete targets for a global reduction in greenhouse gas emissions by 2012. Its underlying principle was 'common but differentiated responsibility'. This laid the heaviest burdens for emission cuts on the greatest producers of greenhouse gases while allowing many countries in the developing world actually to increase emissions to facilitate economic development. Kyoto therefore involved a highly technical and complex set of processes, but its main elements can be distilled. The signatories were divided approximately between those from the global North and those from the South. The developed countries are classified as Annex I states (because they were listed in the first annex to the Protocol). These Annex I states are required to accept specific targets for reductions on a country-by-country basis. The targets amount on average to about five per cent less than their emissions in 1990 (though, importantly, this excludes emissions from international air and sea transport). The underdeveloped countries are Non-Annex states and, as minimal emitters at the time of signature, they are exempted from specific reduction targets. They are however given financial incentives to participate in emission reduction projects embraced by the Clean Development Mechanism (CDM).

Kyoto is described as a 'cap and trade' arrangement. A novel – and controversial – clause in the Protocol allows Annex I states to ease their own pace of reduction by gaining carbon credits from Non-Annex countries through financing CDM projects in them. Alternatively, Non-Annex countries can themselves initiate such projects, for which they receive carbon credits which they can then sell on for financial gain. Annex I countries are required to submit annual reports on their greenhouse gas emissions. National targets would be enforced by 'fines' for those in default which would require them not only to make up the shortfall but face increased targets in future years as well.

The problems with the Kyoto compromise, for that is what it was, are fairly evident. They point up the inherent difficulties in reaching workable multilateral regulation in a voluntary setting. The very limited nature of the commitment required from the Non-Annex states in the global South are striking. But as most of these (though not all, as we will see) had a low carbon footprint at the time of Kyoto, it was understandable. It was in line with the determination, present right from the pioneering Stockholm Conference, that environmental regulation must not strangle desperately needed economic development in the South. More difficult was the 1990 baseline for future reductions. The targets were based on comparative percentages and not absolute emissions. This threatened to penalize those Annex I states, such as the Nordic countries, which had already made advances in environmental control before 1990. Their targets would be likely to be more difficult to meet than those in countries which had been less responsible in their industrial emissions before Kyoto.

The Protocol's lightness of touch on Non-Annex countries proved to be the most controversial aspect of the arrangement – or at least the one around which discontents crystallized. Unsurprisingly, observers of the process paid closest attention to the position of the United States. While the American delegation signed the Protocol it was not ratified by the administrations of either Bill Clinton or George W. Bush. In a political system highly vulnerable to lobbying by sectional interests, Congress came under irresistible pressure from high-emitting industries. Legislators were persuaded that implementation of the Protocol would threaten America's comparative advantage in a globalized economy. This position was bolstered by the fact that neither China nor India, despite their surging industrial outputs, were Annex I countries. Yet at the time the Protocol was opened for signature China was second to the United States in country-based calculations of carbon emissions – and authoritative estimates suggest that it moved into first place during 2006. The American position was shared by Australia's conservative government. The European Union, however, both collectively as an institution and individually as sovereign states, embraced the Protocol. So, finally in 2004, did Russia, after initially refusing ratification. Russia's compliance was especially important as it triggered the mechanism by which the Protocol came into legal effect. This could only follow ratification by at least fifty-five states which between them were responsible for at least fifty-five per cent of greenhouse gas emissions. With Russia signed up, the United States was left as the only permanent member of the Security Council with no timetable in place for the ratification of the Protocol. China announced its adherence in 2002 but this was an inexpensive gesture; as a Non-Annex country it was exempted from any meaningful limits on its emissions.

The narrative of the American rejection is interesting in what

CO_2 EMISSIONS (MILLION TONNES) BEFORE AND SINCE KYOTO

(Based on data from Energy Information Administration)

	1997	2006	% Change
World	21,020	29,195	+28
US	5591	5903	+7
China	3133	6018	+51 (since 1996)
Russia	1482	1704	+5
India	887	1293	+35
Europe (EU)	568	5860	−1 (EU enlarged)

it reveals about the nature of enforcement in a voluntary setting. Washington's position did not come without consequences. United States prestige suffered as a result of its apparent unilateralism. It was particularly damaged under the Bush administration when it was clear that the president himself and his immediate circle were especially hostile to any form of global accountability. Within the United States several individual states passed their own anti-emission legislation in line with Kyoto requirements. To drive home the message of internal dissent, Al Gore, Clinton's vice-president at the time of the Kyoto negotiations, became a powerful public voice for climate action, in particular through the vehicle of his film, *An Inconvenient Truth*. The debate sharpened when the Nobel Committee awarded the 2007 Peace Prize jointly to Gore and the UN Intergovernmental Panel on Climate Change. In short, the costs of unilateralism, of departure from the global consensus, though they may be indirect, can be considerable. An awareness of this no doubt helped determine that in his first days in office in January 2009 President Obama made a considerable effort to signal a change in America's position on greenhouse emissions. Tellingly, perhaps, these moves still fell short of any firm commitment to sign up to the Kyoto Protocol itself.

At the beginning of February 2007 the IPCC produced its Fourth Assessment Report in which it stated baldly that the evidence for potentially catastrophic global warming was now 'unequivocal'. In response, the then French president, Jacques Chirac, proclaimed the Paris Call for Action, urging a renewed global commitment to confront the situation. Specifically, he proposed the replacement of UNEP with a new and more powerful United Nations Environment Organization. Forty-six UN member states associated themselves with the Call for Action. Significantly, however, the largest emitters of greenhouse gases, China, the United States, Russia and India, were not among them. In what may have been an attempt to rescue some prestige while setting targets more acceptable to American interests, the Bush administration attempted to move the debate away from the United Nations. The Washington Declaration of February 2007 brought together the United States and its Western allies along with Russia, China, India and Brazil. In this apparent alternative to Kyoto all participants would agree to meet specific targets. These would however be non-binding. There was no structural difference in this plan between developed and developing countries. The initiative was greeted with widespread scepticism, with many dismissing it as a transparent attempt to subvert the Kyoto process. The absence of the UN from the initiative both heightened these suspicions and denied the Declaration any real international legitimacy despite the obvious weight of the superpower which sponsored it. Long before the arrival of Barak Obama in the White House at the beginning of 2009, the Washington Declaration had been quietly forgotten.

NORTH VERSUS SOUTH ON EMISSION REDUCTION

In India I need to give electricity for light bulbs to half a billion. In the west you want to drive your Mercedes as fast as you want. We have "survival" emissions, you have lifestyle emissions. You cannot put them on the same basis. I am trying to give a minimal commercial energy service, whereas you are not prepared to give up any part of your affluent lifestyle to give up consumption patterns.

Shyam Saran, Indian special envoy on climate change
to the UN – interview with the *Guardian*, 2008

In the meantime, attention shifted emphatically back to the United Nations at the end of 2007 when 192 national delegations gathered on the Indonesian island of Bali. The purpose of the meeting was to consider what was to be done after the end of the Kyoto process in 2012 when the five per cent greenhouse gas reduction target would supposedly be met. The Bali conference followed the alarming IPCC Assessment Report which predicted nothing short of a global climate disaster if immediate steps were not taken to reverse global warming. The Arctic was warming at twice the rate of the global average and the shrinking of its ice cap would have major climatic effects. Extreme weather events were already being recorded throughout the world. Entire island states were in danger of being submerged under rising sea levels. African crop yields, already inadequate for the continent's needs, would be halved. The gross domestic product of the world as a whole would shrink by at least five per cent.

These bleak predictions set the tone of the Bali meeting and many delegations responded accordingly. Australia, now with a new government, announced that it would move immediately to ratify the Kyoto Protocol. The failure of the previous government to do so, which left Australia isolated in the UN and beyond with only the United States for company, had in fact been an issue in the recent election. Bali was not without its theatricality. In an emotionally charged speech the delegate of Papua New Guinea – many of whose islands are at risk of disappearing through sea level rise – denounced American selfishness. At a critical point the senior UN climate change official chairing the meeting, Yvo de Boer from the Netherlands, broke down in tears in the face of Chinese accusations that he was mishandling the negotiations. Despite – or perhaps because of – this high drama an agreement was salvaged from the threatened wreckage. Once again, the intangible but powerful pressure that the United Nations can exert on its members to find common ground was in evidence.

The main purpose of Bali was not so much to reinvigorate the Kyoto process or to track its progress, but to begin negotiations for Kyoto's successor regime. It was, in the words of

Secretary-General Ban Ki-moon, to 'advance a negotiating agenda to combat climate change on all fronts' in order to reach a firm agreement by 2009. Kyoto set targets through to 2012, but negotiations and planning for the next phase beyond this was likely to be a lengthy and difficult process and the end of 2007 was hardly too early to begin it.

In many ways the Bali meeting demonstrated the strengths and weaknesses of the entire environmental project of the United Nations. The outcome – described in the favourite metaphor of contemporary diplomacy as a 'roadmap' – was the result of behind-the-scenes deals between delegations and negotiating brinkmanship. Depending on the perspective, this was a tribute to 'the spirit of flexibility' of the national delegations (Ban Ki-moon) or a map that 'failed to give a clear destination' (Friends of the Earth). At a purely political level the cooperation of the United States in the process of forward planning – albeit last-minute, dramatic and under extreme pressure – was a considerable victory. But the price of this was the deferring of difficult decisions. No specific emission targets were set. A proposal from the European Union that industrialized countries should commit to emission reductions of twenty-five to forty per cent by 2020 was rejected out of hand by the US (along with Canada and Japan). But the final text of the conference did accept the basic principle that 'deep cuts in global emissions will be required to achieve the ultimate objective'. This, given past positions, was a meaningful advance.

The most difficult elements of achieving agreement were left to 2009 when the UN convened a further – inconclusive – conference in Copenhagen. Most important among these elements were: first, the level of binding emissions targets for industrialized countries; second, the commitments required of developing industrial countries; and third, the nature of carbon trading arrangements. It remains to be seen whether the strategies of negotiated compromise and pragmatic delay, often very successful in other areas of the UN's work, turn out to be simply misjudged niceties in this most pressing and time-dependent of global priorities. One worrying element in the longer narrative of emissions control is that the world convened in Copenhagen in an utterly changed economic climate from that at the time of Kyoto. The deep global economic crisis, which appeared with shocking suddenness in the second half of 2008, changed the context of the debate. Anything likely to threaten the survival, let alone the growth, of the industrialized – and the industrializing – economies was unlikely to find favour among those countries most vulnerable to economic slump. The United States and China, which are by far the two most significant players in attempts to reduce emissions, have always been very conscious of and sensitive towards the impact of controls on their industry-dependent economies.

When the definitive history of the first century of the United Nations is written sometime after 2045, its work for the global environment will certainly have a central place. The sheer immensity of current threats will ensure this. Virtually all the 'sectoral' responsibilities accepted by the UN at its inception – security, development, law – are touched by it. Human security is threatened not just by man-made conflict, but by man-made environmental disaster as well. The global environment is interwoven with social and economic development. How else are essential protective and restorative measures to be put in place other than through the framework of international law?

The environment was an area in which the founders of the UN appeared uninterested and over which they had no real concerns. Yet over the past three decades it has risen ever higher in the organization's agenda. The UN's first centenary history then will certainly give prominence to the environment. But how will its performance be assessed? Here as in all areas, the UN must try to win collective goods from individual interests. Nowhere have the difficulties in this endeavour been clearer than in its attempts to tackle the challenge of climate change – perhaps the greatest of all environmental threats yet faced by the inhabited world. Its success or failure in this will be crucial to its second centenary history in 2145. Of course, failure may mean simply that there will be no one here to write such a history.

8

Taking stock: reform and the future

Demands for the reform of the United Nations have been a constant theme in the organization's evolution virtually since the Charter was first signed in 1945. Along the way significant change has taken place. In 1965, for example, the non-permanent membership of the Security Council was expanded from six to ten, and in 2006 the Human Rights Council was created as a new principal organ. Pressure for change is constant, and it comes from a multiplicity of sources which often have conflicting priorities and which view reform in quite different ways. The progress of institutional reform – or, as some would say, the lack of it – highlights the central tension that characterizes the UN as an institution and that has been continuously emphasized throughout this book. There is an inescapable stress in the balance of authority and interests between the institution on one hand and on the other its sovereign independent member states which both regulate it and are regulated by it. The contradictions at the heart of this relationship reach back as well as forward, into the most fundamental debates about the past achievements of the United Nations and about its future shape.

The dilemmas of reform

Having provided the main impetus to the establishment of the United Nations in the mid-1940s, four decades later the United

States led a gathering swell of criticism in the West of its efficiency and performance. Since the 1980s successive US administrations, Democratic as well as Republican, have pressed for administrative reform within the Secretariat to eliminate waste and tackle inefficiency and corruption. Simultaneously, emerging powers such as India and Brazil have bridled at a Security Council with a veto-empowered permanent member-ship which apparently sets in stone the balance of world power at the end of the Second World War.

Meanwhile small states have consistently sought to amplify their own voices along the UN's corridors of power through democratic reform of the General Assembly. Against this small state pressure in turn there is set the complaint of more populous countries that the one-member-one-vote arrangement in the Assembly (based on the venerable principle of sovereign equal-ity) is simply undemocratic. As things stand, India with a population of over a billion has the same voice in the General Assembly as Iceland with little over 300,000 citizens. It may be recalled that this apparent democratic deficit was high on the list of concerns of the Soviet Union when the UN was being formed. At that time Moscow fought to expand its single seat in an organization awash with hostile Western delegations, most of which represented much smaller populations than that of the USSR. But there is yet another twist to this issue. There is the argument that many large states (though fewer than in the past) have forms of government that fall short of acceptable demo-cratic standards. Should, for example, the chaotic, unrepresenta-tive and barely existing government of the Democratic Republic of Congo really have more say in global governance than the soundly democratic government of Luxembourg simply because it has about seventeen times the number of people living within its borders?

There are two inconvenient but stubborn facts facing those advocating fundamental democratic reform. First, at the level of the Security Council, existing permanent members are no more inclined to vote for the loss or dilution of their long-standing special position than the proverbial turkeys are to vote for Christmas. Second, pressure for the democratization of the UN system as a whole comes up against the inconvenient truth that the major financial costs of the organization are borne by the larger states of the global North. These countries have no national interest in dispersing power to the smaller – poorer – states of the South; in other words, they are keenly aware of the relationship between the tunes played and the source of the piper's pay.

In the 1990s the end of the paralysis imposed on fundamental institutional change by East–West rivalry re-energized the reform debate. Secretary-General Kofi Annan in particular was anxious to move the process forward during his period in office between 1997 and 2006. His engagement with the issue was due in part to intensified pressure from sections of the membership for reform as the contours of the post-Cold War world began to arrange themselves. But the historical milestone of the turn of the millennium added a psychological impetus for reform as well. As a public marker of his personal commitment to change, immediately on taking office in 1997 Annan created a new post of under-secretary-general for reform. Since then successive panels, commissions and ad hoc groups have presented wish-lists for change. Most of these begin to founder as they attempt to navigate the deep waters of vested interests among both the membership and the employees of the organization. There has therefore been only scant change in the form of tangible reform as a result.

In September 2000, at a special opening session of the General Assembly attended by many more than the usual tally of heads of state and government, the United Nations Millennium Declaration (UNMD) was launched. This took the form of an Assembly resolution which ranged widely over the world's

KOFI ANNAN'S REFORM AGENDA: MAJOR REPORTS

1997	*Renewing the United Nations: a Programme for Reform*
2002	*Strengthening the United Nations: an Agenda for Further Change*
2004	*High-level Panel on Threats, Challenges and Change*
2005	*In Larger Freedom: towards Security, Development and Human Rights for All*
2006	*Investing in the United Nations: for a Stronger Organization Worldwide*

ills – insecurity, underdevelopment, environmental degradation, the absence of human rights – and the challenges facing the UN in tackling them. The final section of the UNMD pointed to institutional reforms necessary to equip the organization to meet these effectively. The world leaders signing the Declaration resolved to accept 'the central position of the General Assembly as the chief deliberative policy-making and representative organ of the United Nations' as well as to 'intensify … efforts to achieve a comprehensive reform of the Security Council'. These ambitions were set out only briefly and in the most general terms in the UNMD but Annan followed up with the appointment of a High-Level Panel on Threats, Challenges and Change chaired by Anand Panyarachun, a former prime minister of Thailand. This reported at the end of 2004 and provided the basis for *In Larger Freedom*, a landmark report on the workings of the UN which made recommendations for reform unprecedented within the organization. The secretary-general presented this to the General Assembly in March 2005.

In Larger Freedom

The wider purpose of *In Larger Freedom* was to reinvigorate the fundamental aims of the United Nations system for the new century. Seizing the moment, Annan discerned 'a yearning in many quarters for a new consensus on which to build collective action [and a desire] to make the most far-reaching reforms in the history of the United Nations so as to equip and resource it to help advance this twenty-first century agenda'. In a strikingly personal introduction he identified his 'own conscience and convictions' as the central inspiration for the recommendations. The report was designed to provide a basis for discussion among the leaders of member governments who would gather for the opening of the General Assembly in September 2005. This would constitute a special World Summit. Also to be known as M+5, it would review progress on the Millennium Goals set five years previously (see Chapter 6). To this end, the major part of the report concerned concrete issues such as poverty alleviation, security and human rights. However, acknowledging that progress in these critical policy areas required a reformed and revived organizational structure, the final part of *In Larger Freedom* was given over to 'Strengthening the United Nations', a change agenda for the institution as a whole.

A key area for reform was the renewal of the Charter itself, which after sixty years was clearly in need of updating. Specifically, the place of some of the UN's historical organs should be reassessed. The Trusteeship Council, inheritor of the League of Nations Mandate system, had been a major actor in the age of decolonization from the 1950s and 1970s but it was now largely redundant. Consequently, Annan proposed that it be formally wound up and references to it removed from the Charter (in effect Chapter XIII in its entirety). Similarly, the high ambition of the UN's original planners in the mid-1940s for a global system of collective security based on enforcement by the permanent members of the Security Council had long since been discredited. Although its failure had originally been blamed on the polarization of world politics during the Cold War, it soon became clear that even without such a fundamentally divided international system the necessary degree of shared commitment could not be achieved in a world of sovereign states. *In Larger Freedom* therefore urged the deletion of article 47 of the Charter which dealt with the Military Staff Committee of the Security Council (composed of the chiefs of staff of the permanent members). The purpose of the Military Staff Committee was supposedly to plan and oversee collective military enforcement but it had never functioned in any meaningful way (see Chapter 3).

The fate of this eminently sensible tidying up exercise reveals the larger problems of UN reform, however. As Charter amendments require the support of at least two-thirds of all UN members, including all the permanent members of the Security Council, the document remained unaltered at the end of the decade. Both the Trusteeship Council and the Military Staff Committee are still in being, if only as constitutional fictions. And, while the Human Rights Council, another proposal of *In Larger Freedom*, does now exist, it appears nowhere in the Charter and in this sense has no formal legal identity.

Annan's recommendations for General Assembly reform started from the fact of the steady decline in its prestige and its 'diminishing contribution' to the UN's overall activities. It is certainly true that the authority and standing of the General Assembly has dwindled gradually from a high point in the 1960s. At that time the United States and the Soviet Union had vied with each other for its political favour and they had frequently trimmed their foreign policies to this end. Resolutions of the General Assembly were treated then as real statements of world opinion on the international issues of the day. But during the

1970s the prestige and the political leverage of the Assembly began to diminish. In part this was due to the increasing economic weakness and political instability of the countries of the global South which comprised the majority of Assembly members by that time. But in part too it was a result of what Western countries began to regard as a growing tendency of General Assembly resolutions to disregard the limits of the achievable; this made the body easier to dismiss as out of touch with the real world. Then, with the end of the Cold War, big power interest in capturing General Assembly support sharply diminished; there was simply no grounds for competition any more. The overall effect was a shift in the admittedly always unequal balance of power further from the General Assembly towards the Security Council.

There was a general retreat in the new millennium from the more utopian demands previously common in Assembly resolutions. But instead of redressing a long-standing problem, this new 'realism' brought a fresh set of difficulties. In contrast to the earlier excess of radical rhetoric, Assembly resolutions now tended to be overly general in focus and concerned with process rather than substance. The internal politics of the United Nations and a focus on the General Assembly within this had somewhat supplanted the visionary statements of an earlier era. This, Kofi Annan felt, was an unreasonable price to pay for consensus. Procedures, he argued, should be streamlined and the General Assembly should concentrate 'on addressing the major substantive issues of the day'. The Assembly should also widen its conception of the political and engage much more with the organs of civil society throughout the world rather than with just the governments of member states. Ultimately, though, little could be achieved without the commitment of these member governments themselves, who had to take a renewed 'interest in the Assembly at the highest level and insist that their representatives engage in its debates with a view to achieving real and positive results'. In this way, although his sentiments were laudable and his call for the reinvigoration of the Assembly eloquent, Annan had to accept that the agent of change here was the member states and not the institution itself. Perhaps unsurprisingly, little progress seems to have been made.

Turning to the Security Council, Annan proposed a rather more concrete sequence of reform. Reaffirming the report of the High-Level Panel on Threats, Challenges and Change presented earlier in 2005, he set out four fundamental principles for Security Council reform. Any changes should:

bring increased involvement in decision-making of those who contribute most to the United Nations financially, militarily and diplomatically;

lead to decision-making based on the input of a more representative range of national governments, especially from the global South;

cause no impairment to the effectiveness of the Council;

increase the democratic and accountable nature of the Council.

In pursuit of this he presented two alternative models – A and B – for a restructuring of the Council (see textbox). Both models would produce a new regionalized Security Council with four geographic divisions: Africa; Asia-Pacific; Europe and the Americas. They would also increase overall membership from fifteen to twenty-four. Each of the four regions would have six representatives which would occupy various classes (or levels) of Security Council member. Neither Model A nor Model B would extend the power of veto beyond the existing five permanent members whose historical position and privileges would thus be secured.

KOFI ANNAN'S ALTERNATIVE MODELS FOR REFORM OF SECURITY COUNCIL REPRESENTATION

Model A

Regional area	No. of states	Permanent seats (continuing)	Proposed new permanent seats	Proposed two-year seats (non-renewable)	Total
Africa	53	0	2	4	6
Asia and Pacific	56	1	2	3	6
Europe	47	3	1	2	6
Americas	35	1	1	4	6
Total	191	5	6	13	24

Model B

Regional area	No. of states	Permanent seats (continuing)	Proposed four-year renewable seats	Proposed two-year seats (non-renewable)	Total
Africa	53	0	2	4	6
Asia and Pacific	56	1	2	3	6
Europe	47	3	2	1	6
Americas	35	1	2	3	6
Total	191	5	8	11	24

The first of the alternative proposals (Model A) would create six new permanent seats without veto power, two each from Africa and Asia and one each from Europe (east and west together) and the Americas. Two-year term non-permanent membership would be increased from ten to thirteen (four from Africa, three from the Asia-Pacific region, two from Europe and four from the Americas). The alternative proposal (Model B) would create no new permanent members. These would remain as before. It would however introduce an entirely new category of non-permanent member with four-year renewable terms. There would be eight of these, two each from the four regions. Additionally, the ten members currently elected by the General Assembly on a regional basis for non-renewable two-year terms would be increased to eleven. The existing geographical categories of these members, which is still shaped by the Cold War, involves a distribution between Africa with three members, Latin America, Asia and Western Europe with two each and the old eastern bloc with one member (Arab states occupy alternately one of the African or one of the Asian seats). The new Model B would see the distribution changed to four African seats, three from Asia-Pacific members, one from all of Europe and three from the Americas.

National interest: the obstacles to reform

Kofi Annan did not reveal a personal preference for either of the models, though he made clear that he regarded the choice between them as a 'vital decision' which could not be postponed. The debate and arguments which followed the publication of *In Larger Freedom* simply pointed up the almost insurmountable difficulties of the journey to a reformed Security Council, however. Between March 2005 when *In Larger*

Freedom was published and the following September when the World Summit opened, individual UN members and groups of members began lobbying in support of positions favourable to themselves.

Only some of that discussion actually focused on the alternative models presented, and that which did, particularly around Model A's proposal for six new permanent members, was far from conclusive. The two seats which would be assigned to Africa should, many assumed, go to Nigeria and South Africa. Each occupies economic, demographic and military positions which place them on a different scale from their neighbours. Moreover, they are located at opposite geographical ends of sub-Saharan Africa. However, the fact that they are both sub-Saharan countries itself raises questions. Africa as a whole is a much larger entity. Egypt and Algeria are prominent African states as well. The allocation of a seat to one of them would not only maintain a trans-Saharan balance, it would also guarantee a permanent presence on the Security Council of a major Muslim state (Nigeria's complex ethnic make-up prevents it being considered as a truly Muslim country). Algeria might be seen as having a weaker claim than Egypt on a number of criteria but its Francophone identity in a predominantly Anglophone continent would go some way to offsetting other weaknesses in its claim. The rivalry between English and French-speaking Africa is often intense and must always be a consideration in the assigning of international recognition. Allocating the African seats to the two Anglophone giants, Nigeria and South Africa, would almost certainly generate resentment – and not just in Africa itself.

The strongest candidates for the two new permanent Asian seats would be Japan and India. Both are major political and economic actors and each occupies a different sub-region and represents quite different cultures. Japan, though, despite being one of the largest contributors to the UN budget, would probably face strong opposition from China on the grounds of what the latter considers to be unfinished wartime business. China's permanent Security Council status – and therefore its veto – could present a major obstacle to Japanese ambitions. India's qualifications include its huge population (the second largest in the world after China), its powerful and rapidly growing economy and its possession of nuclear weapons. Other Asian states would have their own claims. Either Malaysia or Indonesia would provide the Council with that crucial Muslim presence. They would also represent the diplomatically and economically important Southeast Asian sub-region.

The most convincing European claim to a new permanent seat is generally agreed to lie with Germany. One of the largest world economies, reunified Germany also has a symbolic historical importance as a political and territorial embodiment of the post-Cold War era. It also has the backing both of France, its traditional ally in the post-1945 European project, and of Britain. Along with strong American support, this gives Germany the active backing of three of the existing five permanent members. If Model B were to be adopted, with its proposal for a new class of eight renewable four-year term members, Europe would have two such seats. This would open the way for the additional membership of either a former eastern bloc state or for a non-European Union or non-North Atlantic Treaty state.

Brazil would seem to have the strongest claim to a new permanent seat for the Americas. It is the largest of the Latin American countries in population, economic power and land area. Yet there is a linguistic issue here as in Africa. Brazil is, uniquely, a Portuguese-speaking state in a sub-continent otherwise dominated by the Spanish language. But, again, if Model B were to become reality, two new states for this region would have a renewable four-year term, opening the way perhaps for Mexico to join Brazil.

Inevitably, discussion ranged far beyond the two models presented by Kofi Annan and it soon became clear that his plea that the matter should be treated with urgency had gone unheard amid a generalized shuffling for position. A General Assembly Task Force on Security Council Reform, created to drive the process of agreement, reported in June 2008 and effectively conceded defeat by identifying several additional models which had emerged among different factions. These were notably self-interested. They included the proposals of the African Group, which wanted two new permanent seats with full veto powers and five new permanent seats without veto specifically for Africa, with a further four for the rest of the world. Against this, the so-called G4, composed of Brazil, Germany, India and Japan, sought six new permanent seats to be distributed, unsurprisingly, in such a way as to meet the ambitions of these states themselves, along with four new non-permanent seats. Then there was the forty-strong Uniting for Consensus group of middle-range powers which rejected any increase in permanent members in favour of a simple doubling in the number of non-permanent members.

In the face of these apparently irreconcilable positions the Task Force settled on a time-line approach which would involve a long and complex process of talks–about–talks within and between groups. This would lead at some point, it was hoped, to the emergence of a consensus. Clearly, no concrete outcome should be expected quickly.

Interestingly, the veto, which along with the composition of its membership has been among the most controversial aspects of the Security Council over the years, has not featured greatly among the more serious debates on reform. The importance of the veto to the Security Council's continuing relevance – indeed to the health, even the existence, of the United Nations as a whole – seems to be generally acknowledged, however distasteful it may be to democratic sensibilities. The dangers to the future of a UN without the Security Council veto may have been at their greatest during the Cold War, but it continues to provide an essential backstop which protects the core national interests of the biggest powers. As such, it remains a non-negotiable asset for those who possess it.

The United Nations: an interim progress report

The labyrinthine complexities of the reform process in the UN and the treacle slow pace of change which results, inevitably draws us towards larger questions about the organization's fundamental purposes and usefulness. The resistance, often fierce, by the UN's own members to change and modernization that common sense would see as both logical and overdue is often presented as symptomatic of the failure of the entire project. Often criticism of the UN idea can be unconsciously self-contradictory, though. It is attacked, sometimes virtually in the same breath, for being both overbearing in its interference in the behaviour of its members and for being unable to impose its will on those members when they depart from accepted norms of behaviour. Confused as such criticism may be, it does cast a light once again on the central dilemma of the UN.

Throughout this brief journey across the organization one central issue has appeared and reappeared. This is the fundamental incongruity of a global institution committed to the regulation of state behaviour founded on the basis of the absolute independence of the very states it seeks to control. The history of the United Nations is in many respects simply a record of the attempt to square this circle. At the end of the journey we have to ask how successful this logic-defying attempt has been.

The first point to be made here is that, regardless of success or failure, the United Nations is in a sense inevitable. If it did not exist it would surely be invented. As we have seen, the evolution of international relations over the past centuries reveals a cycle in which the collective management of the state system has become more marked at each turn. Repeatedly, major pressures in the system have led to its breakdown in general wars in the aftermath of which new, ever more elaborate attempts at regulation have appeared. The Thirty Years War ended with the Treaty of Westphalia in 1648 and the principle of state sovereignty. The Napoleonic Wars ended with the Congress of Vienna in 1815 and the Concert of Europe. Then, in perhaps the most crucial turn of the cycle, the First World War ended with the Treaty of Versailles and the creation of the League of Nations – the first truly modern global organization. It would have been unthinkable that the Second World War could have ended without a further advance in this cycle of global regulation.

However historically determined the existence of the United Nations might be though, we can still speculate on the shape of the world without it. Perhaps the most pressing counterfactual here would concern peace and security – the primary preoccupation of those who created the organization. Clearly, the UN has not been successful in its supreme ambition to replace a world of national securities with one of collective security. This was the central area in which the UN was to succeed where the League had failed, but in the event it has achieved little more than its maligned predecessor. The initial alibi of the Cold War and the impossibility of collective action in a polarized world was blown away when, after the fall of the Berlin Wall and the end of the Soviet Union, the states of the world showed no more enthusiasm for abandoning control over their own security.

But the idea of an overarching design for world security is only part – though admittedly a huge one – of the UN's contribution to international security since the Second World War.

Certainly the more modest ventures of peacekeeping and armed humanitarian intervention have had their own dramatic failures from Bosnia to Angola and Somalia but overall, this type of military venture has been a success. Hundreds of thousands if not millions of Cypriots, Mozambicans, Liberians, East Timorese and inhabitants of other countries around the globe lived rather than died – or at least lived more securely than they would have done in the absence of UN military action. And the global consequences of the escalation of conflicts in Africa, Asia and the Middle East which was in the event prevented or controlled by UN intervention can only be guessed at. Other well intentioned actors may have involved themselves in these conflicts if the UN had not existed, of course, but with what legitimacy and therefore at what political risk? At the end of the 1990s when the UN's military failures were particularly in evidence there was a short-lived vogue for denouncing intervention as somehow unnatural, a counterproductive distortion of the life-cycle of conflict. A prominent cheer-leader for this position was the controversial American commentator Edward Luttwak, who argued with some eloquence in an influential article that we should just 'give war a chance' as the best route to durable peace. But it is perhaps not too cheap a shot to observe that Luttwak and his followers would assuredly have felt otherwise if it had been their lives that hung on the presence or absence of blue berets and white armoured cars.

Less direct but nevertheless important contributions were made by the UN in other areas of security. Such arms control and disarmament measures that the superpowers were willing to participate in during the Cold War would probably have come about in some form anyway; these arrangements will always reflect the self-interest of those who agree to them. But the UN, with its underpinning of international legitimacy and authority was able to offer a superstructure within which agreements could be worked out and implemented in the most expeditious way. The UN's absence here may not have been fatal, but it would have been a significant drag on the arms control process.

A similar defence of the United Nations can be offered in the areas of law and environmental protection. International law existed long before the UN had ever been thought of and would assuredly have existed and developed in its absence. But without the UN it would almost certainly develop more slowly in most areas and perhaps not at all in some. The world, in short, would be even less ordered and less cooperative in its attempts at self-regulation. The late twentieth and early twenty-first centuries have presented us with a unique set of problems to solve which are truly transnational in nature. Global resources and the critically important problems of the Earth's ecosystem cannot be confronted by a few states, regardless of their relative importance. Only a proactive global organization can have even the remotest chance of confronting these problems. The prospects for success in this are far from guaranteed; but without the United Nations or something very like it, they simply would not exist.

The great tectonic shift in the modern world brought about by the end of empire and the ensuing explosion in the number of countries in the world would also, of course, have taken place with or without the United Nations. Pressure for change in both colonies and imperial capitals was becoming irresistible by the mid-twentieth century. But what earthquakes were mitigated or avoided altogether – in the Middle East, in Asia, in Africa – by the existence of the UN? By direct intervention where necessary or simply by providing through the fact of membership a confirmation and guarantee of statehood, the United Nations eased the massive adjustments, both local and global, forced on the world by the end of empire.

Against these virtues, the sins of the UN, though many and varied, are for the most part minor. Administrative incompetence and pockets of petty corruption exist. The UN would be truly unique as an organization, not of this world indeed, if they did not. No body of its size and certainly none with its defining commitment to the participation in its management of all nations with their unique value systems and political cultures could be otherwise. From this perspective the remarkable thing perhaps is not the incompetence and low-level misbehaviour of some UN staff but the efficiency and honesty that characterizes the greater part of its activities.

Unavoidably, the discussion returns to the central tension between a regulatory organization and the absolute independence of the states it has to regulate. The greatest supposed failures of the UN – whether genocide in Rwanda, or the apparently inexorable process of man-made climate change – invariably turn out to be in reality failures by states which refuse to be managed by the organization they themselves created for that very purpose. The UN, like any inter-governmental organization, can only work within the limits of the mandate and powers that it is given by its members. At times indeed it is difficult to avoid the cynical conclusion that the real purpose of the UN for many of those members has been to take the fall for their own national failures of global vision and commitment. Blaming the UN is a convenient distraction from shortcomings of government. This is, after all, a phenomenon with a considerable pedigree going back at least to the 'failures' of the League of Nations in the 1930s.

The famous dictum, credited to Alexis de Tocqueville, that 'in a democracy the people get the government they deserve', has a resonance here. Perhaps we can say that the nation-states of the world likewise get the global organization they deserve. Or perhaps, in the United Nations, they may in truth have more than they deserve.

Notes

1. http://avalon.law.yale.edu/20th_century/wilson14.asp
2. http://avalon.law.yale.edu/20th_century/leagcov.asp
3. http://avalon.law.yale.edu/wwii/atlantic.asp
4. http://www.un.org/aboutun/charter/
5. http://news.bbc.co.uk/1/hi/world/middle_east/3661976.stm_
6. Security Council Resolution 84, 7 July 1950. Found at: http://daccess-dds-ny.un.org/doc/RESOLUTION/GEN/NR0/064/97/IMG/NR006497.pdf?OpenElement
7. http://un.org/peace/reports/peace_operations/
8. http://www.un.org/largerfreedom/
9. 'The Nurnberg Trial,' 6 F.R.D. 69,1946
10. General Assembly Resolution 260(III), 9 December 1948. Found at: http://www.un-documents.net/a3r260b.htm
11. http://untreaty.un.org/cod/icc/general/overview.htm
12. http://daccess-dds-ny.un.org/doc/RESOLUTION/GEN/NR0/152/88/IMG/NR015288.pdf?OpenElement
13. http://unesdoc.unesco.org/images/0012/001219/121999e.pdf

Further reading

Chapter 1

Armstrong, David, Lorna Lloyd and John Redmond, *International Organization in World Politics* (Palgrave, 2004)

Bennet, A. LeRoy and James K. Oliver, *International Organization: Principles and Issues* (Prentice Hall, 2001)

Kissinger, Henry, *A World Restored: Metternich, Castlereagh and the Problems of Peace 1812–1822* (Orion, 2000)

van Ginneken, Anique, *Historical Dictionary of the League of Nations* (Scarecrow Press, 2005)

Walters, F.P., *A History of the League of Nations* (Greenwood Press, 1986)

Chapter 2

Boutros-Ghali, Boutros, *Unvanquished: a US–UN Saga* (Random House, 1999)

Luard, Evan, *A History of the United Nations: Vol. I The Years of Western Domination, 1945–55* (Macmillan, 1982)

Russell, Ruth, *A History of the United Nations Charter* (Brookings Institute, 1958)

UN Department of Information, *The United Nations Today* (UN, 2008)

Urquhart, Brian, *Hammarskjöld* (Bodley Head, 1973)

Chapter 3

Blix, Hans, *Why Nuclear Disarmament Matters* (MIT Press, 2008)

Bourantonis, Dimitris, *The United Nations and the Quest for Nuclear Disarmament* (Ashgate, 1993)

Bull, Hedley, *The Anarchical Society: a Study of Order in International Relations* (Macmillan, 1977)

Claude, Inis, *Swords into Plowshares* (McGraw Hill, 1984)

Hastings, Max, *The Korean War* (Pan, 2000)

Larus, Joel (ed.), *From Collective Security to Preventive Diplomacy* (Wiley, 1965)

Richardson, R.C., *A History of Disarmament and Arms Control* (Continuum, 1992)

Sarooshi, Dan, *The United Nations and the Development of Collective Security* (Cambridge University Press, 2000)

White, N.D., *Keeping the Peace: the United Nations and the Maintenance of International Peace and Security* (Manchester University Press, 1997)

Chapter 4

Bellamy, Alex, et al., *Understanding Peacekeeping* (Polity, 2010)

Boutros-Ghali, Boutros, *An Agenda for Peace: Preventive diplomacy, peacemaking and peace-keeping* (1992): www.un.org/Docs/SG/agpeace.html

MacQueen, Norrie, *Peacekeeping and the International System* (Routledge, 2006)

The Responsibility to Protect. Report of the International Commission on Intervention and State Sovereignty (2001): http://www.iciss.ca/report-en.asp

UN Department of Peacekeeping Operations: www.un.org/Depts/dpko/dpko/

UN Department of Political Affairs: www.un.org/Depts/dpa/index.html

Wheeler, Nicholas, *Saving Strangers: Humanitarian Intervention in International Society* (Oxford University Press, 2000)

Chapter 5

Convention on the Prevention and Punishment of the Crime of Genocide (1948): www.un.org/millennium/law/iv-1.htm

Halstead, Peter, *Human Rights* (Hodder Arnold, 2008)

Joyner, Christopher, *The United Nations and International Law* (Cambridge University Press, 1997)

Lowe, Vaughan and Malgosia Fitzmaurice, *Fifty Years of the International Court of Justice* (Cambridge University Press, 2007)

Schabas, William, *An Introduction to the International Criminal Court* (Cambridge University Press, 2007)

Statute of the International Court of Justice (1945): www.icj-cij.org/documents/index.php?p1=4&p2=2&p3=0

Statute of the International Criminal Court (1998): http://untreaty.un.org/cod/icc/statute/romefra.htm

United Nations Treaty Collection: http://untreaty.un.org/

Universal Declaration of Human Rights (1948): www.un.org/en/documents/udhr/

Chapter 6

Convention on the Rights of the Child (1989): http://209.85.229.132/search?q=cache:4bU_Pu7f3dwJ:www2.ohchr.org/english/law/crc.htm+convention+of+the+rights+of+the+child&cd=7&hl=en&ct=clnk&gl=uk

Loescher, C.I., *UNHCR: the Politics and Practice of Refugee Protection into the 21st Century* (Routledge, 2008)

Luard, Evan, *A History of the United Nations: Vol. II The Age of Decolonization, 1955–65* (Macmillan, 1989)

Marshall, Katherine, *The World Bank* (Routledge, 2006)

Murphy, Craig, *The UNDP* (Cambridge University Press, 2006)

New International Economic Order (1974): http://www.un-documents.net/s6r3201.htm

Toye, John, et al., *The UN and Global Political Economy* (Indiana University Press, 2004)

United Nations Convention Relating to the Status of Refugees (1951): http://www.un.org/millennium/law/v-14.htm

Vines, David and Christopher Gilbert, *The IMF and its Critics* (Cambridge University Press, 2009)

Chapter 7

Declaration of the United Nations Conference on the Human Environment 1972 (Stockholm Declaration): www.unep.org/Documents.multilingual/Default.asp?DocumentID=97&ArticleID=1503

Henson, Robert and Duncan Clark, *The Rough Guide to Climate Change* (Rough Guides Ltd, 2008)

Imber, Mark, *The Environment and International Relations* (Routledge 1996)

Intergovernmental Panel on Climate Change (IPCC) Fourth Assessment Report (2007): www.wmo.int/pages/partners/ipcc/index_en.html

Johannesburg Action Plan 2002 (Plan of Implementation): www.un.org/esa/sustdev/documents/WSSD_POI_PD/English/POIToc.htm

Rio Declaration on Environment and Development 1992 (Agenda 21): www.unep.org/Documents.Multilingual/Default.asp?DocumentID=78&ArticleID=1163

Timmons Roberts, J. and Bradley C. Parks, *A Climate of Injustice* (MIT Press, 2007)

Chapter 8

Bourantonis, Dimitris, *History and Politics of UN Security Council Reform* (Routledge, 2005)

Clements, Kevin P. et al., *The Center Holds: UN Reform for 21st Century Challenges* (Transaction, 2006)

Franda, Marcus F., *The UN in the Twenty-First Century* (Rowman and Littlefield, 2006)

Luttwak, Edward N., 'Give War a Chance', *Foreign Affairs*, July–August 1999

A More Secure World: Our Shared Responsibility. Report of the High-Level Panel on Threats, Challenges and Change, 2004: http://www.un.org/secureworld/

In Larger Freedom: towards development, security and human rights for all. Report of the Secretary-General, 2005: http://www.un.org/largerfreedom/

United Nations Millennium Declaration, 2000 (UNMD): www.un.org/millennium/declaration/ares552e.htm

Index

A Beginner's Guide to Nato

9781851683536
£9.99/ $14.95

A comprehensive yet concise and accessible introduction to the history, role, activities and future challenges facing NATO. Despite predictions of its imminent demise, NATO is in fact more prominent than ever in international affairs, and this readable introduction will prove essential not only for the general reader, but also for the growing numbers of students on International Relations courses, and for service personnel in NATO and elsewhere.

"Knowledgeable and able, this introduction covers the major developments of NATO's post-Cold War evolution in an accessible manner."
Anand Menon – Professor of Politics, Birmingham University

JENNIFER MEDCALF is Lecturer in Politics at the University of Bath, England. She has taught and written widely on the subject of international affairs, and convenes courses for the armed forces, in addition to providing consultations for the media on NATO and related issues.

Browse further titles at
www.oneworld-publications.com

A Beginner's Guide to The Middle East

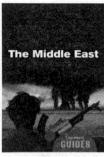

9781851686759
£9.99/ $14.95

This compact book by the University of Oxford's leading expert is stuffed with historical background, real-life examples, profiles of key figures from Nasser to Gadaffi, and even popular jokes from the area. *The Middle East: A Beginner's Guide* will captivate tourists, students, and the interested general reader alike.

"Masterly. A comprehensive and succinct overview." **Hugh Pope** – Former Middle East Correspondent for *Reuters, Wall Street Journal,* and the *Independent*

"The best book on the modern Middle East. Perfect not only for students but for any reader. It is balanced, authoritative and easy to follow. A perfect introduction to this troubled region." **Christopher Catherwood** – Author of *A Brief History of the Middle East*

PHILIP ROBINS is Reader in Middle East Politics at the University of Oxford. He is the author of *A History of Jordan* and has previously worked as a journalist for the BBC and the *Guardian*.

Browse further titles at
www.oneworld-publications.com

A Beginner's Guide to Crimes Against Humanity

978-1-85168-601-8
£9.99/ $14.95

Using examples ranging from the genocides in Darfur and Rwanda to the use of torture in the 'war on terror,' Jones explores the progress made in toughening international law, and the stumbling blocks which prevent full compliance. Coherent and revealing, this book is essential for anyone interested in the well-being of humanity and its future.

"Jones has written a much-needed conceptual overview and call to action which will wake people up to the worst of which humanity is capable." **Charli Carpenter** – Assistant Professor, Department of Political Science, University of Massachusetts Amherst

"A remarkable book that is immediately accessible for the novice in the field, or students, and yet also engages with its topic in intellectually interesting ways for the more seasoned reader." **James Gow** – Professor of International Peace and Security, King's College London

ADAM JONES, Ph.D., is Associate Professor of Political Science at the University of British Columbia Okanagan, Canada.

Browse further titles at
www.oneworld-publications.com

A Beginner's Guide to Democracy

David Beetham offers new insights into the role of the citizen and how large corporations affect democracy as well as contemplating the future of democracy in the developed and developing worlds.

978-1-85168-363-5
£9.99/ $14.95

"Beetham's book should stimulate anyone, beginner or expert, who is interested in the survival and renewal of democracy in the era of globalization." **Peter Singer** – Author of *The President Of Good And Evil: Taking George Bush Seriously*

"A strong and shrewd mixture of analysis and polemic…If more was not to come, I would call this the author's crowning achievement." **Sir Bernard Crick** – Advisor on citizenship to the UK government

DAVID BEETHAM is Professor Emeritus of Politics at the University of Leeds, a Fellow of the Human Rights Centre at the University of Essex, and Associate Director of the UK Democratic Audit.

Browse further titles at
www.oneworld-publications.com